Of Man and God

Of Man and God

by
Alfred Pomerantz

PHILOSOPHICAL LIBRARY
New York

Table of Contents

Introduction	Monads and Entities	1
	Identity	3
	Perception, Impression and Conception	7
	Conceptual Entities	9
	Substance and Essence	14
Chapter I	God, Gods and Idols	19
II	Trinity	34
III	The Messiah	54
IV	History and Historicity	75
V	The Historicity of Jesus Christ	87
VI	Names of Monads and Entities	95
VII	The Name of God	103
VIII	Invoking the Name of God	108
IX	Receiving Christ	112
X	"His Own Received Him Not"	127
XI	Man's Love	134
XII	An Allegory of Time and a Clock	146
XIII	Institutions and Attitudes	
	a. The Communist Party	149
	b. The Roman Catholic Church	160
XIV	The Teachings of the Roman Catholic Church	167
Conclusion		176

INTRODUCTION

Monads and Entities

So far as human intelligence has been able to determine, every single thing in the universe exists in itself, regardless of whether it has been perceived by any animate being. Each thing is objectively real: were all existing minds obliterated, a thing might continue to exist in itself.

Solipsists have contended not only that unperceived things do not exist in themselves, but that things perceived by the five senses are nonexistent, the five senses being merely extensions of the imagination. This problem tormented Descartes, who strove to formulate a premise upon which he could build a sound system of epistemological methodology. The premise he ultimately formulated was that the one thing he could be certain of was the existence of his own mind: *"I think, therefore I am."*

My purpose is not to expound arguments either for or against present-day solipsists, heirs of Descartes' work only in part, since they agree with the validity of his premise while rejecting the edifice of deductions he built upon it.

If nothing extrinsic to myself exists, moreover, it is futile for me to write about nonexistent things for the benefit of a nonexistent reader. I therefore begin my discussion hoping that the reader is not a creature of my imagination, but an animate monad with a life of his own.

1

By the word "monad" I mean a spirit, soul or mind complete in itself. Unique, independent and indivisible, it cannot be joined with other minds in the manner chemical elements, for example, can be compounded with other elements to form compounds. A monad can be joined with matter, however, to form an animate entity. Each animate entity is, in fact, a compound consisting of a monad and a body; not every monad, however, is a component of an animate entity.

Several classes of monads have been conceived of as having existed:

(a) An existing soul that has never been a component of an animate entity.

(b) A defunct soul (one no longer existing) which, during its existence, was never a component of an entity.

(c) A defunct soul, during its existence a component of an animate entity.

(d) A soul currently a component of an animate entity, by which the body is exclusively animated. I call this compound an extant entity. Such a soul resides in the body in the sense that its knowledge is conditioned by the perceptions conveyed to it by the body's senses. Its conditioning is therefore a function of the location of the body within which it resides: It is *in loco*—local—not *in ubi*—in many places simultaneously.

(e) A soul formerly a component of an animate entity, but continuing to exist after the death of the body. Of course, the compound—or entity—has ceased to exist from the moment the soul was released from it.

(f) A soul that has been in turn a component of several entities. The process by which a soul migrates from one body to another is called "the transmigration of souls." The reality of this process is devoutly believed in by millions in the Orient, but is generally derided in our part of the world.

(g) A soul simultaneously a component of more than one entity.

(h) A defunct soul once compounded with a body but, with that body's death, no longer existing. Probably most of the people of the Occident believe—although they do not like to admit this even to themselves—that any soul compounded with a body is destroyed when that body dies.

(i) A soul both *in loco* and *in ubi*. The Trinitarian Christians believe God has always been a ubiquitous soul but that for a time He manifested Himself as a man, dwelling among other men; that during the two days between the body's death and resurrection He was separated from the body; and that simultaneously with the resurrection of the body He was re-compounded with it. Many of them also believe that the devil is a ubiquitous soul who joins himself with bodies to form entities.

(j) A soul rejoined with a body that died and was resurrected. The New Testament relates that a man named Lazarus was resurrected from the dead. His soul at one time was in this class of monads.

Some monads may be categorized in more than one class; for example, at one time a monad may have been a member of class (d), at another time class (e).

Identity

An identity is a physical part of an entity which affords the possibility of the entity's being recognized through perception and memory. Each human entity has many identities; each identity consists of a combination of form and matter. It is not necessary to perceive an entity itself, however, to have an impression of some of its identities. Reproductions such as pictures, statues and voice recordings are means of conveying identities to one's senses without perception of the actual phenomena.

Since a human entity—a person—has many identities, various persons may recognize him by different identities or different combinations of identities. One person may recognize him by his face (which in itself consists of many identities); a blind man may recognize him by his voice.

There are methods for concealing identities, such as masquerading with garments, or growing a beard. Such methods are used by persons who wish to be disguised and by those impersonating others. The Bible relates that Jacob, with garments made from the skins of goats, was able to simulate the hairy body of his elder brother, Esau, thus receiving from his blind father, Isaac, a blessing intended for his brother.

All the identities of an entity are continuously changing, however, so that one's recognition of the person depends on how greatly the familiar identities have altered since the last perception, plus one's recollection of those identities. If, in addition to undergoing natural changes, an entity's face has become disfigured through violence or disease, its alteration might be great enough to render it unrecognizable to some persons who remember it as it was. If the alteration of the face has been so great as to render it unrecognizable to everyone who knew it, the original identity—the face as it was before its great alteration—has become defunct as a means of recognizing the entity. Should an entity known to a blind man only through its voice lose that voice, then the blind man will be completely unable to recognize it; consequently, he will no longer know the entity through his knowledge of the defunct identity. It is said that Helen Keller, who is both blind and deaf, knows her intimate friends by touch. If, then, the skin of one of her friends were to deteriorate through disease, or if the features of this person were to become altered in an accident, she would no longer know this friend.

Again, the word "know" is used to signify the ability to recognize an entity through perception either of the actual entity or of a reproduction of some of his identities. But the

4

word "know" is also used to convey mutual acquaintanceship. For example, an ordinary person might say that he knows President Johnson, in the sense that he is capable of recognizing him; he would also say that he doesn't know him in that he and the President do not enjoy a mutual acquaintanceship. People also use the word "know" to indicate understanding a person—what he is. I shall use the word "know," however, only to indicate the knowledge of identities.

Regarding a monad that is not joined with any physical body, it is possible for it to know us, but not for us to know it. Furthermore, an extant entity that we do not presently know but that we know about is the equivalent of a monad who has never been joined with a physical body, so far as our present knowing of him is concerned. For example, from a plaque on a building we may know that the name of its architect is John Doe. But if we do not know an entity named John Doe, so far as our present knowing of him is concerned, he might as well be a disembodied spirit.

On the other hand, we may know an entity without knowing either who or what he is. When we talk about *who* a person is, we mean his function or functions in the social scheme of things: the president of a railroad; the father of so-and-so; the right-fielder of the Chicago White Sox baseball team. When we talk of *what* an entity is, we mean his nature and accomplishments, regardless of who he is: a chess player; a gourmet; a liar; a thief; a philosopher. Of course, in some instances who an entity is is also what he is, as in the case of the right-fielder of the Chicago White Sox. But when we say that so-and-so is a liar, we certainly are not talking about who he is.

Our knowledge of who and what an entity is can never be absolute. Just as we can know only some of a person's identities, we can know who and what he is only to a limited degree. For example, the New Testament relates that the people of Nazareth knew Jesus was the carpenter's son; that

5

his mother was Mary and his brethren James, Joses, Simon and Judas (Matthew 13:55). But they did not know he was the Christ. John 1:10 states, "He was in the world, and the world was made by him, and the world knew him not." *He,* according to Trinitarian Christian theology, being Jesus, the words "the world knew him not" can only mean that all people did not know certain things *about* Jesus, not that they did not know him. Of course, people in China, who never saw him, did not know him, but certainly his neighbors in Nazareth knew him.

An entity's works are not identities. We cannot know an entity through his works alone. Sometimes, however, his works can be correlated with his identities. A newly discovered musical composition does not in itself convey any identity of its composer, but sometimes we can correlate its style with that of an identifiable composer. For example, the publishers of the composition *The Bee* give the name of its composer as François Schubert. But the style of this composition is unmistakably that of the well-known Austrian composer, Franz Schubert, a defunct entity whose one-time extant identities are known through pictures. It is evident that *The Bee* was published originally in France, for "François" is the French language equivalent of the German language name "Franz." And even if the composition had been published under a name completely dissimilar to that of Franz Schubert, the cognoscenti still would have known the composition to be that composer's work. If, however, Franz Schubert had never been a monad joined with a body, reproductions of the identities of which are still extant, the composition in itself could not convey to us any of this composer's identities. In short, the works of an entity are not identities, for they are not part of that entity's physical makeup. They are, rather, the entity's "footprints on the sands of time."

Perception, Impression and Conception

A perception is the immediate awareness of an object conveyed to a monad by one or more of his senses, plus his differentiation between this and other objects.

An impression is a monad's recollection of a perception. A conception is an association of an impression of one object with another object. An impression is usually changeable, probably because it is unconsciously distorted by conceptions. Often different impressions are mixed until they bear little resemblance to their perceptions, so that an impression of an entity's face or voice more and more misrepresents the identities that were actually perceived. Although I have impressions of heads having only one ear, if I were to think of, say, President Johnson as having only one ear, this thought would be a conception. Nevertheless, having seen the President, my recollection of him *in toto* is an impression. In most cases impressions are accurate enough for the purpose of recognition, even though the identities recognized may have altered.

In the Frick Art Collection in New York City, three paintings hang side by side: El Greco's *St. Jerome* and Holbein's *St. Thomas More* and *Sir Thomas Cromwell*. The circumstances under which these paintings were produced illustrate perception, impression and conception. Since St. Jerome lived in the fourth century, it is evident El Greco, who painted him twelve centuries later, had no impression of him. This painting, therefore, represents a conception. On the other hand, St. Thomas More and Sir Thomas Cromwell were contemporaries of Holbein. It is probable that these men posed for Holbein. If so, these portraits are reproductions of perceptions. If, however, Holbein painted their portraits from memory, these portraits represent impressions.

7

Statues and paintings of saints dead for centuries are artistic productions representing conceptions. Many such statues in Rome are said to be representations of New Testament figures; sculpted before the Christian era, however, they were thought at that time to represent pagan gods. In the pre-Christian era, the statue of St. Peter under the cupola of the Church of St. Peter was regarded as the statue of the Roman god Janus. According to the New Testament, Jesus gave the Apostle Peter the keys of the kingdom of heaven. "And I will give unto thee the keys of the kingdom of heaven" (Matthew 16:19). When Romans were converted to Christianity, the statue of Janus, with keys in his hand, was thus particularly suited to represent Peter. A Roman Catholic textbook admits: "There are no doubt conspicuous exceptions, but perhaps all things considered the average Catholic would have a much truer conception of the saints were all the painted and sculptured representations of them sunk to the bottom of the deep blue sea."

Philomena is the name given to the monad whose earthly remains were discovered on May 24, 1802, in the catacomb of Priscilla, in Rome. The bones were those of an adolescent girl. Before 1802 no one had heard of this monad. But since the skull was fractured, it was concluded she had been killed for her faith, and her bones were regarded by many as those of a martyred saint.

Recently the Sacred Congregation of Rites of the Roman Catholic Church declared that the widespread opinion that Philomena is a saint in heaven is in error. An Associated Press dispatch from Rome, dated April 18, 1961, stated that "all statues and pictures of Philomena have been ordered removed, or no longer venerated." *Time* Magazine, April 28, 1961, had an article stating: "Cardinal Cushing had distributed 800 statuettes of St. Philomena to Dover (Massachusetts) Catholics when he read in the paper that the Vatican's Sacred Congregation of Rites had stricken St. Philomena, the virgin martyr, from the roster of saints. Instead of dedicating the red brick church in Dover as St. Philomena's, the Cardinal dedicated it as the Church of the Most Precious Blood." In the New York *Daily News,* April 21, 1961, a picture appeared of Rev. Joseph Boyle carrying a statue of "former St. Philomena" from the altar of the Dover, Massachusetts, church.

The removal of this statue from a Roman Catholic church indicates the monumental confusion that results from naming statues which are only representations of conceptions. Why should a statue named Philomena be singled out for removal? The act implies this statue is actually a representation of an entity named Philomena. Since Roman Catholic authorities admit no one knows what Philomena—or many true saints, for that matter—looked like, why not simply change the name of a statue called Philomena to that of a true saint, as with Janus?

Conceptual Entities

A conceptual entity is one which exists only in the human imagination; it cannot be perceived by the senses. The unicorn is often portrayed in paintings and tapestries. It has a single horn in the center of its head, and the body of a horse. The individual members of this conceptual animal are not conceptions. But because of this peculiar admixture of animal members, the unicorn is conceptual.

The unicorn can be thought of as an artistic analogue of the characters in novels and plays. The authors of fiction are not delineating the characters of real entities they have known or read about; they are creating characters having characteristics in common with real people. What is conceptual, however, is the aggregate of a given fictional character's qualities.

9

Nevertheless, characters of fiction are often considered stereotypes. In *The Merchant of Venice,* for example, Shakespeare was attempting to illuminate the damaging effects of racial and religious prejudice, dramatized in the conflict between the Jew, Shylock, and the Christian, Antonio. To illustrate his theme, he could just as well have laid the scene in the East Indies and created a Chinese as the antagonist and an Indonesian as the protagonist. Unfortunately, although seeking revenge for real or imagined wrongs is not a characteristic peculiar to Jews, the author's arbitrary use of a Jew demanding a pound of flesh has served to reinforce the Christian world's generally unfavorable opinion of Jewish character. Moreover, if it is assumed that the plot is true to life (which it is not) and if the preponderantly Christian audiences conceive of themselves as behaving in the same manner as Shylock's Christian antagonists, they do not consider the revenge they vicariously take on Shylock to be excessive. This illustrates the all-too-common human failing of seeing the mote in another's eye while ignoring the beam in one's own.

Furthermore, there are several passages in *The Merchant of Venice* which conclusively prove that inaccurate opinions can exist in a mind even as great as Shakespeare's when its contact with the world is limited. We know that the Jews were barred from England from the time of their expulsion by Edward I in 1290 until their readmission by Cromwell in 1657. It is therefore understandable that Shakespeare's opinions regarding Jews originated in hearsay. No doubt he read parts of the Bible, but he was grossly ignorant of Jewish history, customs and traditions; and he confounded some Christian customs with those of the Jews. For example, the custom of invoking the intercession of saints is Christian, not Jewish. I do not believe that in all of Jewish history any Jew has ever invoked the assistance of the patriarchs Abraham, Isaac and Jacob, except perhaps in the secret cabalistic

10

rites of the rabbis of the Middle Ages: "For Thou art our Father; For Abraham knoweth us not, And Israel doth not acknowledge us; Thou, O Lord, art our Father" (Isaiah 63:16). The appeal to a patriarch, put into the mouth of Shylock by Shakespeare:

> O father Abram, what these Christians are,
> Whose own hard dealing teaches them suspect
> The thoughts of others!

is therefore typically un-Jewish.

At another point, Shylock, seeing his Christian adversary, Antonio, says in an aside, "I hate him for he is a Christian." I do not believe it is characteristic of Jews to hate Christians as such. They may hate them for other reasons, but not for having a faith other than Judaism. The Jews jealously guard their religion as a gift from God given exclusively to them; consequently, they do not proselytize, as do the Christians. Thus, although they undoubtedly think other religions are inferior to their own—as do all religionists—it would be absurd for them to resent the Christians' practice of Christianity or the Moslems' practice of their religion. In this passage, Shakespeare, living in a milieu of religious bigotry, evidently assumed that all religious peoples were bigoted.

Shylock alludes twice to his tribe: "Tubal, a wealthy Hebrew of my tribe"; and "Cursed be my tribe, if I forgive him." By putting these words into the mouth of a Jew, Shakespeare shows his ignorance of Jewish history. For the tribes of Israel have long ceased to exist as separate organizational entities: the descendants of these tribes have become so assimilated that, with the exception of the Levites, they no longer think of themselves as members of any particular tribe. To my knowledge there are no Levitical organizations. Aside from their few liturgical functions, the Levites' distinction is only honorary. This situation goes back to the pre-Christian era.

11

It is also unlikely that a devout Jew would know the New Testament story of devils being conjured into a herd of swine (Matthew 8:31-32), which Shylock refers to:

> Yes, to smell pork; to eat of the habitation
> which your prophet the Nazarite conjured the devil
> into.

And even if he knew the story, he certainly would not accept it as authentic—which evidently Shylock does—for the Jews do not believe in the historicity of events related in the New Testament. The prohibition against eating pork predates the Christian era by at least a thousand years, and has nothing to do with the devil, who is not mentioned in the Old Testament books of the Law. Shakespeare's imputing the cause of the Jews' abstaining from eating pork to an event allegedly occurring during Jesus' life on earth is another illustration of the poet's ignorance of Jewish history.

Indeed, authors have made all kinds of mistakes in writing about peoples and customs they know little about. For example, the author of the first chapter of the Gospel of Luke confounded Jewish and Gentile customs when he wrote that the relatives and friends of a Hebrew priest, Zacharias, and his wife, Elizabeth, at the time of the circumcision of their son, John the Baptist, called him Zacharias after the name of his father (Luke 1:59). This author was evidently ignorant of the Jewish custom of giving new-born children either original names or the names of deceased relatives. It is unthinkable that orthodox Jews would name a child after a living relative; certainly, no such event is related in the Old Testament.

Perhaps the naming of children after dead relatives is a way of expressing an unconscious desire to reincarnate the spirits of departed persons who may have been greatly loved or with whom past differences have not been settled.

For example, a man who has lost his father may unconsciously try to project a father-image upon his son. And as the child grows, much trouble can be caused by the father's attempted imposition of the grandfather's character upon him. For the grandfather's character may have been vastly different from the child's innate character.

In any case, the author of Luke 1:59 certainly fabricated a fictional event, correlating it with an actual event—the circumcision of John the Baptist. Indeed, intertwining conceptual events—mere creations of the imagination—with actual past occurrences is probably a universal fault of historical works.

Using the example of Shakespeare's creation, Shylock, I have been discussing conceptual entities. I now turn to a discussion of conceptual character as it relates to real entities. In their thought, men are continually assigning spurious attributes to the mentalities of persons they know, and divesting them of attributes truly theirs. No doubt there is always a great difference between an observer's subjective appraisal of the mentality of an entity he knows and its actual mentality. For an observer is always prejudiced by his own peculiar faculties and experience. Indeed, different monads probably always interpret differently things they observe commonly. Carlyle said: "To Newton and to Newton's Dog Diamond, what a different pair of universes; while the painting on the optical retina of both was, most likely, the same!"

Mankind are all more or less Don Quixotes in their tendency to confound and dilute their sentient experience with second-hand information acquired through reading or hearsay. Having once espoused a theory, tacitly or openly, men often deny even to themselves evidence which obviously confutes that theory. Like ostriches burying their heads in the sand, they ignore actualities which do not support their theories, desires and aspirations. The theoretical, conceptual facets of the mind vis-à-vis the realistic ones, and the per-

13

petual debate between the two, are contrasted in the behavior of Don Quixote and his constant companion, Sancho Panza.

Is it not true many divorces are brought about because people do not "see" each other? They only partially know each other's mentality? Disillusionment in marriage often results from the discovery that spurious attributes have been associated with one's mate. So that after many years one comes to say, "I see you now for the first time." The discovery of undesirable traits in one's mate is often more of a blow to his self-esteem than disappointment in the once-admired mate. For this discovery has proved his judgment poor. It often happens that the most intense hatred is directed at those in whom we have discovered attributes we had not previously suspected were theirs. We feel we have been fooled.

Spurious deeds, also, are often imputed to entities, as is always the case in a murder trial. Both prosecuting and defending attorneys know the defendant, but do not "see" him in the same light. If the defendant happens to be innocent, the prosecutor has imputed to him a spurious deed, regardless of the actual facts he knows about him.

Substance and Essence

The quality, form and size of a body comprise its physical substance. But what is the difference between physical substance and physical essence? Two pennies may be consubstantial in essence. They are not, however, of the same essence, since you can do what you desire with one—spend it—and at the same time do something else with the other one—jingle it in your pocket. Thus, two consubstantial things are not of the same essence, for they are not one and the same. Another illustration: two glasses of water of the same quantity and form are consubstantial in essence; they are the same substance but not the same essence, for if the water in one glass is combined with other chemicals, it will no longer exist as water, even though the water in the second glass does not change. Third illustration: two apples may be consubstantial in essence, but they are not of the same essence, for the continued existence of one is not dependent on whether or not the other has been consumed.

If water is poured from one container into another having a shape different from the first, the water's quality and volume remain the same; its substance and essence have both changed, however, since its form has changed.

A monad's mental substance consists of all its mental attributes in both quantity and quality. But in contrast to physical substance, mental substance has no form.

Do either the physical or mental essences of a human entity remain unchanged as time passes? Aristotle said that an oak has something in it of the acorn from which it grew. An oak cannot grow from a loadstone or a chicken's egg, but only from an acorn. An oak and the acorn from which it grew are the same living body, although obviously not of the same essence. Similarly, a man is not of the same essence, either mentally or physically, that he was as a boy. Nevertheless, he is an outgrowth of his boyhood; he is the same living organism. Of course, changes in the physical and mental makeup of an entity are not always a result of natural development. They are sometimes caused by violence, sickness or mental disturbance induced by environmental influences. It is also undoubtedly true that the changing physical essence of an entity reacts on its mental essence, and vice versa.

The changing of an entity's essence is well illustrated by a story told in connection with Da Vinci's celebrated painting, *The Last Supper*. It is said that Da Vinci painted Jesus first, and that several years later he unwittingly used as the model for Judas Iscariot the same person he had used as the model for Jesus. Evidently, as a result of some devastating experience, the model's countenance had altered to such an extent that even Da Vinci, who must have been an expert physiognomist, did not recognize it.

Let us imagine the changing physical and mental essences of monads as being represented by plots in Cartesian coordinates on two graph papers of indefinite size. The ordinates of one represent physical substance and the other mental substance; the abscissas in both represent time. Such imaginary graphs are no doubt mathematically unfeasible, since the relationship between various ordinates of an actual graph can be only quantitative. Nevertheless, conceptually these graphs will serve to illustrate the relationship between the substances of monads.

The mental substance of every monad that has ever existed is plotted as a function on the graph of mental substance. The physical substance of any entity or entities with which each of these monads has been joined is plotted on the graph of physical substance. Theoretically it is possible for two functions to cross each other or have common ordinates at different times. However, since through experience we are almost certain that no two entities are ever consubstantial, either physically or mentally, and that every entity's physical and mental substances are continuously changing, it is almost certain that no two functions can have a common ordinate either at the same time or at different times. But the relationship between a monad's substance at one point in his life to his substance at another time is represented by two points on the same function, despite the fact that this function cannot be formulated mathematically.

If, upon seeing a man we have not seen since he was a boy, we mistake him for another, it is because having known only some of the points on the function of his physical substance, we have been unable to formulate this function. Usually,

16

however, if the natural development of an entity has not been scarred by physical violence, we can, upon suddenly seeing him after a long passage of time, relate his present ordinate of physical substance with former ordinates, thus determining them to be in the same function. In brief, we recognize the entity.

On the graph of physical substance, the zero ordinate represents, of course, physical nonexistence. Thus, if the physical body with which a monad has been joined dies, the monad's function of physical substance drops vertically to zero at the moment of death, for it is no longer joined with that body. If, however, this monad survives the demise of its body and is thereafter eternally constant in mental substance, its graph of mental substance does not drop vertically to zero at the moment of death; it is thereafter represented by a horizontal line extending infinitely to the right from the point in time of its physical death. Moreover, if it is true, as some believe, that after an entity's physical death, the monad which was a component of this entity not only survives, but is also reincarnated in another body, then this monad's function of physical substance will be zero in its ordinate only between those limits of time starting from the first entity's death and ending when the monad is reincarnated in its new body. If it is true, as others believe, that each monad of defunct entities shall one day be reunited with its resurrected body, then such a monad's ordinates of physical substance will be zero only between those limits of time starting with physical death and ending with resurrection.

Chapter 1

GOD, GODS AND IDOLS

The word "god" connotes any monad superior to man in wisdom and strength and having the ability to partially or totally dominate man's physical or spiritual life.

Polytheists are those who believe in the existence of many gods, none of whom are omnipotent. Some polytheists believe in the existence of both male and female god-monads.

Monotheists, among whom are the adherents of the three principal religions of the Western world—Judaism, Christianity and Mohammedanism—are those who profess belief in the existence of one supreme god, omniscient and omnipotent, creator of all spiritual and material things. Justin Martyr, one of the early fathers of Christianity, about the year 150 c.e. defined the supreme god as "that which is and always continues to be the same, and is the cause of the existence of all other beings." I believe the present leaders of the three branches of Western monotheism would agree with this definition of the supreme god.

In English language works of monotheists and in translations into English of works of non-English-writing monotheists, "god," when connoting the alleged supreme god, is capitalized. In such works all pronouns referring to God are of the masculine gender and are also capitalized. Some writers say that Biblical words such as "Jehovah," "Jesus Christ," "The Eternal," "The Ancient of Days," "The Lord," and "The Lamb" are really names and titles which God gave Himself. For this reason, these writers capitalize pronouns for which such words are antecedents. I, however, shall use capital letters only in pronouns for which the antecedent word is "God."

The three principal branches of Western monotheism agree that God was always a spirit-monad. But the Christians, in contradistinction to the Jews and Moslems, believe not only that He joined Himself with a human body, but that this incarnation of the divine monad and its transitory appearance among men on earth is the central fact of history.

But let it not be thought that in the past all Christians thought of themselves as monotheists. For example, Marcion (second century C.E.) believed the two most powerful gods were completely independent of each other, neither created by the other, neither supreme. Marcion was a Christian in that he believed in the divinity of Jesus. But he claimed the god who was the father of Jesus was not the same monad as the one that created the universe. As we shall see in my discussion of Trinity, although Marcion's doctrine of two independent gods has been anathematized by all Trinitarian Christian sects of the present day, belief in the existence of two independent super-monads is actually far more compatible with present-day Christian thought than the Christian clergy dare admit even to themselves.

Many people in the Western world who are not affiliated with any of the three great faiths professing monotheism are nonetheless monotheists. For example, those who call themselves deists are monotheists. They believe in the existence of a supreme monad, creator of the universe, whom they call "God." But they believe that the Bible, with all its inconsistencies, is not His revealed word and imputes to Him attributes and deeds merely conceptual.

Pantheists are monotheists who believe that the universe, with all its material and spiritual things, is, by extension, part of God. In the seventeenth century, Spinoza, who became a pantheist, believed not in *creatio ex nihilo* (creation out of nothing), but rather that the universe is an excrescence of God. Spinoza, a Jew by birth and upbringing, thus came to dissent from many of the doctrines of orthodox Jewry. Having incurred the displeasure of the elders of his synagogue, he was excommunicated in July, 1656, after refusing to recant.

Those who call themselves atheists say that all gods are conceptual monads—that "man created God." But it is nonsense for theists to call atheists "Godless," an epithet one often hears nowadays. If God exists, He must have created atheists as well as theists.

The question of God's existence has been argued from time immemorial. I am not completely convinced of His existence. I even suspect that professed believers are in reality as doubtful as I, since they continually find it necessary to bolster their faith with arguments and "evidence." One does not try to prove to one's self what one knows to be true. Moreover, if religious leaders could prove God exists, their religions would be sciences, not faiths. Do not theists resent an atheist because he boldly expostulates what they secretly suspect is true? Apparently many feel compelled to argue for His existence to "play it safe," fearing that if He does exist He will punish those who do not profess belief in His existence. My own belief is that the creator who limited the intelligence of people cannot possibly resent their ignorance of His existence. Therefore, I echo Pythagoras' statement, "Of the gods I do not speak because I cannot know," and confine my discussion of gods to an analysis of what has been said about them by those who have claimed they know. I will assume the monotheists are right—that one supreme monad, God, creator of all things, exists.

According to the Old Testament, a collection of ancient books canonical in both Judaism and Christianity, there

21

exist other gods besides God. In the Bible—both Old Testament and New—some of these gods are called angels.

The Jews and Christians claim that the Old Testament was the first book that proclaimed monotheism to the world. They base this claim on the famous verse, "Hear O Israel: The Lord our God is one Lord" (Deuteronomy 6:4), and on the story of the creation of the world by God (Genesis, chapter 1). Scholars now have evidence that the story of the creation in Genesis is of Babylonian origin and that it was interpolated in this book after the Jews returned from their Babylonian exile to Palestine in the sixth century B.C.E. Moreover, there is nothing in the words "The Lord our God is one" implying the existence of one omnipotent monad who created all things. The Hebrew word which is here rendered "our God" in English should have been rendered "our god," for in Hebrew there are no capital letters. And in most English translations of the Old Testament, the words "the Lord" are substituted for the name "Jehovah," which is a transliteration from Hebrew, whenever this name appears (over six thousand times). Therefore, Deuteronomy 6:4 should properly read: "Hear O Israel: Jehovah our god, Jehovah is one."

The ancient Israelites in Palestine were not more monotheistic than the small nations surrounding them. The Israelites believed a god existed who called himself Jehovah and patronized them exclusively. The other small nations were also exhorted by their religious leaders to believe one god was patronizing them. For example, the Philistines, contemporaries of the ancient Israelites, thought a god named Dagon was *their* national patron.

The Israelites did not think Jehovah was the omnipotent creator of the universe. Judges 1:19 says, ". . . the Lord [Jehovah] . . . could not drive out the inhabitants of the valley, because they had chariots of iron." Further, there is evidence in the Bible that certain ancient peoples, including

22

the Israelites, believed in the existence of the patron gods of other nations. Naomi, an Israelitess, speaking to her daughter-in-law, Ruth, said, "Behold, thy sister-in-law is gone back unto her people, and unto her god." And Ruth, a Moabitess, replied, "Entreat me not to leave thee . . . thy people shall be my people, and thy God my God" (Ruth 1:16-18). (Here again, the translators have erroneously rendered the word "god" as "God.")

The statement "O Lord [Jehovah], thou art my God [god]" (Psalms 31:15) could have been written only by a person who believed Jehovah to be a particular monad of a general class. For if the Hebrew word here rendered as "God" connoted only one monad, then "Lord" and "God" would be synonymous. If this were the case, the psalmist's statement would be as foolish as that of a small child who says, "O Father, thou art my dad."

Implicit in the words "the Lord our God" is the notion of exclusive possession. Americans speak of President Johnson as "our President." But if President Johnson were president of all peoples, all over the world, none of them would speak of him as "our President," as though he were exclusively theirs. In Lessing's poetic drama, *Nathan the Wise,* appear the following words:

> "His God—for whom he fights!" Can God be owned?
> What sort of God were he whom man could own—
> Who needs defenders?

The only answer to this question is that those who speak of "our God," although they may not realize it, impute to the word "God" a meaning other than that of the supreme monad, creator of all things.

That the Mosaic Law, including the Ten Commandments, is actually polytheistic is evident from the jealousy imputed to Jehovah in it: "Thou shalt have no other gods before

Me . . . for I the Lord thy God [god] am a jealous God [god]" (Deuteronomy 5:7-9). It is plain that the writer believed in the existence of many gods struggling against each other. The original writers evidently had no notion about a supreme monad; if they did, they certainly did not think Jehovah was He. How could the creator of the universe be jealous of gods who were either real monads created and controlled by Him or conceptual monads residing in idols?

Idols are statues carved out of wood or stone, resembling men or animals. The ancient polytheistic peoples believed that their patron god's spirit resided either in one idol or in many idols made to simulate each other as much as possible. They believed that the attention of their god could be evoked by addressing any of these statues directly. If, for example, a people was united by the belief that its patron god's spirit resided in statues of cats, then holy places with such statues were constructed within reach of all the faithful.

In our own time, in such religions as Buddhism and Catholicism, whose adherents claim they were founded by monads in human form, statues allegedly simulating the religions' founders as they were when they walked the earth thousands of years ago have been placed in many locations. These statues facilitate prayer to these monads, who are believed to be eternally extant in spirit. In the Catholic churches there are also statues supposedly simulating the human bodies of such monads as the Virgin Mary and other saints.

The evil of idol veneration, particularly in Catholicism, is that the mind of the idolater becomes conditioned to believing in the possibility of the coalescence of human bodies with God Himself. The way is thus opened for many an unscrupulous person to claim he is God. Indeed, this has happened many times in Christendom. Let me quote from Sir James Frazer's *The Golden Bough:*

Christianity itself has not uniformly escaped the taint of these unhappy delusions; indeed it has often been sullied by the extravagances of vain pretenders to a divinity equal to or even surpassing that of its great founder. In the second century, Montanus the Phrygian claimed to be the incarnate Trinity, uniting in his single person God the Father, God the Son, and God the Holy Ghost. Nor is this an isolated case, the exorbitant pretensions of a single ill-balanced mind. From the earliest times down to the present many sects have believed that Christ, nay God himself, is incarnate in every fully initiated Christian, and they have carried this belief to its logical conclusion by adoring each other. Tertullian records that this was done by his fellow Christians at Carthage, in the second century. . . . The adoration of each other was customary among the Albigenses, and is noticed hundreds of times in the records of the Inquisition at Toulouse in the early part of the fourteenth century.

In the thirteenth century there arose a sect called the Brethren and Sisters of the Free Spirit, who held that by long and assiduous contemplation any man might be united to the deity in an ineffable manner and become one with the source and parent of all things, and that he who had thus ascended to God and been absorbed in his beatific essence, actually formed part of the Godhead, was the Son of God in the same manner with Christ himself, and enjoyed thereby a glorious immunity from the trammels of all laws human and divine.

The placing of statues of Jesus in Roman Catholic churches has in a way been a drawback to the Church, for races other than the Caucasian do not accept the Caucasian race's conception of the God-man. In Roman Catholic churches of China, statues of the Virgin Mary holding the child Jesus are those of a Chinese woman holding a Chinese child. The Roman Catholic missionaries in China, faced with the xenophobia of the Chinese, were forced to compromise what they believed to be the truth: that the God-man was a Caucasian, not a Mongoloid.

The human heart seems to long for communion with perceivable matter joined with the spirit powers that be. The ancient Israelites were just as addicted to this all-too-human folly as were their enemies. In spite of the Second Commandment's prohibition of the making of graven images and the admonitions of their prophets, the Israelites were continually "backsliding" (to use Jeremiah's metaphor of social reaction) into idolatry. The patron god, Jehovah, was believed by many to reside in the brass serpent Moses had made in the wilderness (Numbers 21:8-9). This brass serpent was not originally meant to be worshiped. Yet it was placed in the temple in Jerusalem built by Solomon and worshiped by many as late as the reign of King Hezekiah in the eighth century B.C.E. Hezekiah finally destroyed it. "He [Hezekiah] removed the high places, and broke the pillars, and cut down the Asherah; and he broke in pieces the brazen serpent that Moses had made" (2 Kings 18:4).

Even the wise Solomon (c. 1000 B.C.E.) became an idolater in his old age (2 Kings 11: 4-8), and in spite of Hezekiah's acts general idolatry continued to flourish in Judah until the reign of King Josiah (638-608 B.C.E.).

The early spiritual life of the Israelites was thus dominated by their struggle to free themselves from the belief in the corporeal presence of Jehovah. It is a maxim that civilizations progress by a series of "two steps forward and one step backward." In this manner the Israelites, although they gradually progressed toward total freedom from idolatry, were periodically backsliding to their old ways. But idolatry among the Jews seems to have been abolished by the time of the Babylonian Exile.

The Second Commandment prohibited the Israelites from making any graven image. But Moses gave them a portable tabernacle, called The Ark of the Covenant, in which the spirit of the national patron god was to reside perpetually. This belief in a sanctuary from which Jehovah could be evoked provided a means of offsetting the abhorrent practice of idolatry. The great drawback of the Ark was its mobility, which rendered it susceptible to capture by an enemy. In the famous battle of Aphek (*c.* 1075 B.C.E.), this is exactly what happened. The Ark was brought from Shiloh in a desperate eleventh-hour attempt to rally the faltering Israelites. When it was captured by the Philistines, the Israelites, thinking that they had lost their god, suffered a complete breakdown of *esprit de corps* and "they fled every man to his tent" (1 Samuel 4:10). This debacle was one of the greatest in the history of ancient Israel (". . . for there fell of Israel thirty thousand footmen"). The Ark was later recaptured, and when Solomon built the temple in Jerusalem (*c.* 1000 B.C.E.) it was placed in the sanctum sanctorum, where it was hidden from the gaze of all except the High Priest, who went into it once a year, on the Day of Atonement, to commune with Jehovah. Apparently its capture by the Philistines at the Battle of Aphek had raised doubts regarding its function as the home of Jehovah. The reappraisal of the Ark which inevitably followed resulted in its losing its status as a perpetual sanctuary and becoming a vessel from which the spirit of Jehovah could be invoked only once a year. A religious revolution had taken place in which the principal seat of Jehovah's august presence was transferred from terrestrial man-made vessels to heaven, away from the arena of human strife:

> The Lord is in His holy temple,
> The Lord, His throne is in heaven (Psalms 11:4).

It is indeed certain that at the time of Herod the Great,

27

during whose reign in Judea the New Testament says that Jesus was born, the Jews had many centuries before thrown off forever the belief that Jehovah, being a spirit in heaven, would manifest himself in any living agency on earth. "The heavens are the heavens of the Lord, but the earth hath He given to the children of men"—a verse widely known among devout Jews—thunders from the 115th Psalm like a theological "East is East and West is West and never the twain shall meet." It is a powerful scriptural refutation of the Christian belief in God's manifestation as a human being on earth.

The conceptual patron gods worshiped by weak nations such as the ancient Israelites and Philistines were actually nothing more than aeges by which the clergy of a nation tried to unify it. The worship of each patron god was indicative only of people unified through their common profession of faith in that god; and his alleged strength was really nothing more than the collective strength this group could muster. If the Israelites won a battle against the Philistines, religious dissidents among them who had been openly skeptical of Jehovah's strength were deterred from defecting to the faith of Dagon, sincere believers were strengthened in their faith, and opportunistic fence-sitters at least paid lip service to him. In short, there was a marked increase in open profession of confidence in Jehovah, indicative of the strengthening of national unity and self-confidence through the defeat of an enemy.

On the other hand, when the Israelites lost a battle, public confidence in Jehovah was shaken. Many "went a-whoring after strange gods," as the Bible puts it (Judges 2:17); and fence-sitters and dissidents defected to the enemy by converting to his religion. When fratricidal wars broke out between the Israelites, with one faction allying itself with a Gentile power, that faction would also go a-whoring after the enemy's god. And when this kind of whoring became the order of the day, even many clergymen, instead of adhering to a cause which appeared hopeless, acceded to public opinion and "went a-whoring" themselves.

W. Robertson Smith, in *The Religion of the Semites*, writes, "When the gods of the several Semitic communities took part in this way in the ancestral feuds of their worshipers, it was impossible for an individual to change his religion without changing his nationality, and a whole community could hardly change its religion at all without being absorbed into another nation." The Israelites' increasing profession of faith in Jehovah during the reigns of the early kings thus indicates their increasing national self-confidence and unity, brought about by continual elimination by war of the peoples surrounding them. Their continual use of the name "Jehovah" to designate their patron god has, indeed, always been a concomitant of their continuity as a distinct group.

The power of the clergy of each national group rose and waned with the degree of public confidence in the god to whom they ministered. It was thus in the clergy's interest to ascribe national disasters such as epidemics and defeats in battle to their god's wrath toward his people for their disobedience, not to his impotence. The Israelite clergy contended Jehovah was more powerful than the enemy gods but that he withheld his support in battle from his people when they did not deserve it.

There is an opinion abroad in the world, particularly among the devout, that one's success is due to one's righteousness and moral superiority and that a personal setback should be followed by self-searching and self-censure. The recent astonishing revision in the American people's self-image is comparable to the self-searching of the ancient Israelites which followed national setbacks; for the recent technological advances of the Soviet Union and the consequent diminution of America's primacy as the world's foremost industrial power has brought about a reappraisal by the American clergy of America's spiritual and moral primacy. Whereas only a few years ago the American clergy were proclaiming America's "spiritual values," present-day shibboleths are our "spiritual bankruptcy," "crass materialism," and "spiritual decay"; whereas previously they trained their guns of moral censure on the world outside America, their sights are now trained inwardly. Still, can it truthfully be said that America is now spiritually decadent, whereas ten years ago she was spiritually rich? Has America's morality really deteriorated so greatly within the short space of ten years?

About 1000 B.C.E., when the Israelites and Philistines still believed in the existence of many national patron gods, the Phoenicians, who were much farther advanced as a nation than either the Israelites or the Philistines, were monotheists. Such a powerful nation had no need for a patron god to fight the gods of other nations. They called the Omnipotent "Baal." Although the word "Baal" was used to name God, the word itself, unlike "Jehovah," is an appellative, and means "master." It was also used as a title of respect; for example, one who owned slaves was titled "Baal." Many passages in the Hebrew scriptures indicate this word was used not only by Phoenicians, but also by Israelites, as a title of authority.

The Phoenicians designated angels by hyphenated names, such as Baal-Zebub (the lord of flies).[1] Baal delegated to each angel a specific power over man or nature.

The Greeks also were monotheists before the Israelites. They believed in the existence of one supreme monad, creator and master of all the world:

O thou! [Jove] from whom the whole creation springs.[2]

In ancient Greek thought, many subordinate monads assisted Jove. These lieutenants of the supreme monad were called "gods":

1 "Baalim" means "angels" ("Baal" is singular) .
2 Homer's *Odyssey*.

On high Olympus, Jove convened the gods;
The assembly thus the sire supreme addressed.[3]

Through an obfuscation of words and ideas, the ancient
Greeks and Phoenicians are generally thought of today as
polytheists. Modern Judaism and Christianity are said to be
monotheistic in that they teach the existence of only one
supreme monad. But they also teach the existence of angels
and devils, immortal creatures with power not as great as
God's, yet superior to man's. Assuming angels and devils
exist, are they not creatures of the same order in nature as the
creatures the Greeks called gods and the Phoenicians called
Baalim? Thus, the ancient Greeks and Phoenicians are called
polytheists only because of their word usage, not through
the correct understanding of their thought.

Jeremiah, a prophet who lived during the period of the
Babylonian Exile, believed that of all the gods of the nations
the only one who actually existed was Jehovah, patron of the
Jews. He further believed that Jehovah was God. In verse
2:11, he shames the Jews for being fickle:

> For pass over to the isles of the
> Kittites, and see,
> And send unto Kedar, and consider diligently,
> And see if there hath been such a thing.
> Hath a nation changed its gods,
> Which are yet no gods?

By "gods which are yet no gods" he undoubtedly means
"gods which are not real monads"—fictitious, conceptual
monads whose names and idols are aeges under each of
which a Gentile people was unified. It is thus evident that
by the time of the Babylonian Exile the prestige of the name
"Jehovah" had increased to the extent that at least some of
the Jews thought not only that this name was that of their

3 *Ibid.*

patron god, but also that their god was God. This was tanta-mount to a complete rejection of the Pentateuchal doctrine of many existing gods who provoked Jehovah to jealousy.

Evidently Jeremiah, who for a time was one of the captives in Babylon, was greatly influenced by his captors, who had been monotheists for a long time. Jeremiah was unwilling to concede that Jehovah, patron god of the Jews, was a conceptual monad. If such an admission had spread among the Jews, it would have brought about their final downfall as a religious group. With their conversion to monotheism during the Babylonian Exile a synthesis had to be effected in which Jehovah would be thought of not only as the patron of the Jews, but also as God. Because of this synthesis, there is in modern Judaism the paradox of the omnipotent creator who is also an exclusive possession. To this very day Jews speak of Jehovah as "our God." In Christianity, as we shall see later in the discussion, there is a similar paradox in that Jesus is called both "our Lord" and "Lord of the universe."

Many present-day Biblical scholars are certain that the first eleven chapters of Genesis were interpolated in the Hebrew scriptures after the Jews were converted to monotheism. In the first chapter of Genesis, which contains the account of the creation, the Hebrew word used to designate God is "Elohim"; the name "Jehovah" does not appear. In the second chapter of Genesis, however, appear the words "The Lord God" ("Jehovah Elohim"). But in other passages of the Bible the word "Elohim" is used to connote beings other than God. For example, in Psalms 8:6 the Hebrew word "Elohim" is rendered "angels" in all English versions of the Bible; and in the famous verse "Thou shalt have no other gods before me" (Deuteronomy 5:7), "Elohim" is the Hebrew word rendered in English as "gods." If the first chapter of Genesis had been extant in the Hebrew scriptures prior to the composition of Psalms 8:6 and Deuteronomy 5:7, certainly the word "Elohim" would not have been used by the writers of these Psalms and Deuteronomy verses to mean "gods" or "angels." The conclusion is inescapable that the early chapters of Genesis, in which the words "Elohim" and "Jehovah" are both used as names of God, were a post-Exilic interpolation. For only then were both thought of as being names of God.

Chapter 2

TRINITY

The Trinitarian Christian position is basically that during all eternity God consists of three monads—the Father, the Son and the Holy Ghost. The three are consubstantial in spirit-essence; and knowing each other's mind, are in perfect harmony and agreement. However, one of the three—the Son —joined himself with a human body and appeared on earth as the human entity, Jesus.

In the Trinitarian Christian mind, belief in the onetime presence on earth of the human incarnation of the Son of God is the proper way of believing in God. And yet St. Thomas Aquinas said, "The knowledge of God by means of any created similitude is not the vision of his essence"; and borrowing the language of Maimonides, the twelfth-century Jewish sage, he also said, "God is incorporeal."

The Trinitarian Christians also believe that the body of Jesus ascended to heaven; that this body still is the Son's habitat; that it is now "on the right hand of God" (1 Peter 3:22); and that eventually it will return to earth—the second coming of Jesus.

It is interesting not only that the Father is physical (for he has a "right hand"), but that the Holy Ghost manifested himself physically in the form of a dove: "And the Holy Ghost descended in a bodily shape like a dove upon him" (Luke 3:22). Now if Jesus was born of the union of the

Holy Ghost with the Virgin Mary ("She was found with child of the Holy Ghost"—Matthew 1:18), then in spirit-essence he must have been the Holy Ghost from the start. If the Son-monad is the Holy Ghost-monad, why are they thought of as two separate monads? And how could the Holy Ghost descend from heaven upon the man Jesus if it had already been manifested in him from the moment of his conception in the Virgin Mary's womb? And if the Holy Ghost—one of the "persons" of the Triune God—was incarnate as a dove, why do not the Christians worship the dove? Furthermore, the Gospel of Luke says that Elizabeth, mother of John the Baptist, was "filled with the Holy Ghost" (Luke 1:41) and that his father, Zacharias, was "filled with the Holy Ghost" (Luke 1:67); and the Book of Acts (Acts 2:4) says that the Apostles were all "filled with the Holy Ghost." If all these persons were filled with the Holy Ghost —the third person of the Triune God—they also must have been manifestations of God. Why are they not so thought of by Christians?

According to Trinitarian Christian belief, Jesus had two natures, one human, the other divine. His humanity exists "in time," his divinity—the monad—"in eternity." His humanity was a creation, and was the messenger transmitting to men the word of his divinity. It was this creation—the body existing "in time"—not the Son of God-monad himself, which shed its blood for the remission of sins. But because the body in which the Son-monad manifested himself suffered for the sins of the world, the Son alone, not the Father or the Holy Ghost, is called the Savior.

Since the human entity, Jesus, with which the Son-monad is joined, ascended to heaven and has not reappeared on earth, no one knows what that body looked like: "Yea, though we have known Christ after the flesh, yet now henceforth know we him no more" (2 Corinthians 5:16). Even if we assume this body to exist in heaven, it is for all practical purposes defunct, for if it were to return to earth in a "second coming" no one could recognize it as the body of the Son-monad. He could just as well come to earth in a body other than that of the first coming and no one would know the difference. Thus, the important thing is not the body in which God appeared "in time" on earth, but that He *is*: "He that cometh to God must believe that he *is*" (Hebrews 11:6).

With regard to the anthropomorphism pervading Trinitarian Christian theology, let me quote from Locke's *Essay Concerning Human Understanding*: "How many amongst us, will be found upon enquiry to fancy him in the shape of a man sitting in heaven, and to have many other absurd and unfit conceptions of him?"

And from Frazer's *The Golden Bough*: "The notion of a man-god, or of a human being endowed with divine or supernatural powers, belongs essentially to that earlier period of religious history in which gods and men are still viewed as being of much the same order, and before they are divided by the impassable gulf which, to later thought, opens out between them."

These remarkable passages vindicate the progressiveness of the complete spiritualization of God, to which the Jews have adhered since the Babylonian Exile, against the partially materialistic Trinitarian Christian notion of God's history, which holds that His spirit has been incarnated in a human body.

As to the nature of God, even the Bible provides evidence supporting Frazer's belief that our present-day notion of Him is not derived from revelation, but rather is the most recent link in a long chain going back to our primeval ancestors' fancies. Our present notion of God is therefore only a stage in a continuing evolutionary process.

Malachi (fifth century B.C.E.), last of the canonical Jewish prophets, believed "Jehovah" was the name of God. Being a monotheist, Malachi taught that Jehovah has always been the same in essence: "For I the Lord [Jehovah] change not" (Malachi 3:6).

Let us examine the Bible to discover whether the character of Jehovah changed or not. A psalmist describes Jehovah as though he were a dragon: "Smoke arose up in his nostrils: and fire out of his mouth did devour" (Psalms 18:9). And Chapter 11 of the Book of Judges relates that Jehovah (who had condemned the offering of human sacrifice to other gods as abominable) himself accepted a human sacrifice. The prophets on the other hand, writing in a more humane age, had a gentler opinion of Jehovah. For example, Isaiah said that Jehovah did not even desire the sacrifice of animals:

> To what purpose is the multitude of your
>   sacrifices unto me?
> Saith the Lord;
> I am full of burnt-offerings of
>   rams,
> And the fat of fed beasts;
> And I delight not in the blood
>   of bullocks, or of lambs, or of he-goats. (Isaiah 1:11)

If Jehovah did not change, why did he command the Israelites to offer sacrifices to him and later revoke this statute? Was it not, according to the Bible, this same monad—Jehovah—who planned to obliterate the Israelites because of their constant complaints of the rigors of their desert wanderings? He was dissuaded from this course only through his colloquy with Moses, who first counseled him that if he reneged on his promise to bring the Israelites to the land of milk and honey, he would become known as a weak, undependable god, then cajoled him as to his "loving kindness" (Numbers 14:11-20).

This passage serves to illustrate that in parts of the Bible gods and men were thought to be of the same order, to use Frazer's words. In fact, it is evident that Moses was immeasurably superior to Jehovah in patience, perseverance and compassion. For it was Moses, a mere man, who had to shoulder the burden of leading the "stiff-necked" Israelites, continually suffering their bitter abuse, while Jehovah, a god, was immune from the sting of man's ingratitude. If one actually believes this story, and also believes that Jehovah is God, he cannot avoid the conclusion that man is capable of rising to a higher degree of moral excellence than that of his creator.

Deutero-Isaiah, who lived during the Babylonian Exile in the sixth century B.C.E. and whose works are combined in one book with the writings of Isaiah I, who lived two centuries earlier, thought of Jehovah as a monad giving enlightenment to all, not just to the descendants of Jacob: "And he said, It is too light a thing that thou shouldst be my servant to raise up the tribes of Jacob, and to bring back the preserved of Israel; but I will also appoint thee for a light to the nations, that my salvation may reach as far as the end of the earth" (Isaiah 49:6). It is thus evident that in spite of the words claiming constancy which Malachi puts into the mouth of Jehovah, the character of Jehovah, as described in the Bible, *did* change from a god patronizing a particular group to a god teaching all mankind.

Frazer says: "Primitive man creates his gods in his own image. Xenophanes remarked long ago that the complexion of Negro gods was black and their noses flat; that the Thracian gods were ruddy and blue-eyed; and that if horses, or oxen, or lions only believed in gods, and had hands wherewithal to portray them, they would doubtless fashion their deities in the form of horses, and oxen and lions." As we have shown, the faith of Israel in its early stages anthropomorphized the character of Jehovah but has never created him in the physical image of man. On the other hand, to this

38

day the Trinitarian Christian mind, which pictures God in the form of a man, seems to be that of the "Primitive man," who, as Frazer characterizes him, "creates his gods in his own (physical) image." The platitude that says "We all believe in one God," often used to "break the ice" in theological discussions between representatives of the three major Western faiths, is therefore highly inaccurate. A more accurate common denominator for monotheists would be "We all believe one supreme monad exists."

In the "Tale of the Three Kings" in Boccaccio's *Decameron* is an allegory pertaining to the question of which of the three monotheistic faiths—Islam, Judaism and Christianity— is the true religion God gave men. The person to whom the question has been put avoids committing himself to a definite answer, saying no one really knows which one of the three is the true faith. To explain his position by allegory, he tells a story about a family heirloom which is handed down through the generations from father to favorite son. Eventually the heirloom is possessed by a man who has three equally deserving sons. To prevent quarreling after his death, he has two rings made, indistinguishable from the original, and shortly before his death he gives each son a ring. After his death the sons find out about the other rings; thus none of them knows for certain whether he possesses the true family heirloom.

This story of the family heirloom that has become unidentifiable through duplication illustrates the foolishness of the desire to cherish relics, such as the Holy Grail, which are said to have played a part in the great events of the past.

The perpetual association of divine doctrines with a transitory physical appearance on earth of the Son of God-monad is even more foolish. Even if it is true that there has been only one human body in which the spirit of God has resided and from whose mouth He promulgated many of His laws and rules of conduct, so far as knowledge of these promulgations is concerned, the efficacy of being aware of this amalgamation of the divine and human in Jesus was limited only to the period of time in which He was earthbound: a person living in Palestine at that time, if properly inspired, would know whom to go to in order to hear the word of God. Since that body has ascended to heaven, however, the generations of Christians who have never known it have been apprised only through hearsay and reading of the word He promulgated from that body as an interlocutor. But even before God manifested Himself in the flesh, some of His promulgations were known to true believers through interlocutors such as the prophets. Certainly He could have continued to instruct men by proxy. Indeed, the instruction of men by God in His human manifestation has served only to confuse them. For many who believe He spoke through the prophets do not believe in His manifestation as a man; consequently, those who believe in the reality of that manifestation are disposed to exalt the doctrines He taught from His human body and to denigrate those He taught when He was just a spirit. Thus, the only plausible reason for God's manifestation as a human entity was for Him to shed the blood of that entity to redeem the sins of the world.

The Christian belief in a divine benefactor of the human race who bears the burden of its sins is rooted in remote non-Jewish antiquity. Aeschylus' dramatic poem *Prometheus* was acted in Athens five centuries before the Christian era. The story of the trial and crucifixion of Prometheus by the ministers of the offended Jove is strikingly similar to the New Testament's story of Jesus' trial and crucifixion by Pontius Pilate.

The early Christians who were converted from Judaism did not believe in the divinity of Jesus. They believed in the Old Testament's precept that God is an invisible spirit. Indeed, this precept is reiterated in the New Testament: "Now unto the King eternal, immortal, *invisible,* the only wise

God . . ." (1 Timothy 1:17) ; "Who only hath immortality, dwelling in the light which no man can approach unto; whom no man hath seen, nor can see . . ." (1 Timothy 6:16); "God is a spirit; and they that worship him must worship him in spirit and in truth" (John 4:24).

It is true that some parts of the New Testament, such as the first chapter of the Gospel of John, seem to strongly intimate the incarnation of God as a man. According to John 20:28, the disciple Thomas called the resurrected Jesus "My Lord and my God." There is no evidence that this Gospel was known before the time of St. Irenaeus, a second-century European Gentile who is the earliest Christian writer to mention the Gospel of John. Indeed, the evidence points overwhelmingly to Irenaeus' pseudepigraphy of parts of it. Also highly controversial is the verse, "For there are three that bear record in heaven, the Father, the Word, and the Holy Ghost: and these three are one" (1 John 5:7) , some theologians believing it to be an interpolation. In some versions of the New Testament it is deleted.

The European peoples who were being converted to Christianity in its early stages had long been accustomed to believe that gods and goddesses have family ties. In the Trinitarian belief of ancient Egypt, the second person of the Trinity was called the Logos, or Word; the third person was the incarnation of the Logos as flesh. The goddess Isis was thought to be a virgin who gave birth to savior Horus through a supernatural cohabitation with the god Osiris. This was a theological forerunner of the Virgin Mary's pregnancy by the Holy Ghost. It seems that after Alexander the Great's armies conquered Egypt (fourth century B.C.E.) his soldiers introduced the religion of Osiris into Europe. To accommodate the time-honored beliefs of the European Gentile converts, who eventually constituted the preponderant part of the Christian church, Irenaeus interpolated "The Word was made flesh" into the fourth Gospel, fraudulently imputing its authorship

41

to John, a disciple of Jesus. It is evident that the original author of this Gospel did not believe Jesus was God: "For my Father is greater than I" (John 4:28).

A fierce controversy was engendered in the early Church between those who believed Jehovah was the only God-monad and the European Gentile converts who had long been conditioned to believe in gods who fathered children consubstantial with them in spirit-essence. During the first three centuries of the Christian era, it was optional for a Christian to believe that the Son and the Father were consubstantial in spirit-essence. The latter belief was certainly not obligatory; otherwise the Arians, a sect of Catholic priests who denied the equality of the Father and the Son, would have been excommunicated for promulgating blasphemous doctrine. Roman Emperor Constantine, in order to bolster the solidarity of the Empire and hasten its religious unity, in 325 c.e. summoned the clergy to a conference at Nicaea and ordered them to resolve the dispute. If in the year 325 the dogma of Trinity had already been officially incorporated into the canon of the Church, it would have been ridiculous to call a conference to resolve a nonexisting dispute. The so-called Nicaean Creed, born of the conference by majority vote and made binding on all Catholics thereafter under pain of excommunication, finally consummated the formal incorporation into the Church canon of the consubstantiality in spirit-essence of the Father, the Son and the Holy Ghost. Constantine the Great, who at the time of the conference had been freshly converted to Christianity, can be justly called the Father of Trinitarian Christianity.

The absorption of this spurious doctrine into the religion which teaches belief in the protagonist of the New Testament, Jesus, thus impelled the clergy to search the scriptures for passages which could be interpreted as validating it. An exegesis was developed holding this doctrine to be implicit in certain passages, such as: "I and my Father are one" (John 10:30) and "Before Abraham was, I am" (John 8:58). The clergy were also forced to incorporate the Old Testament into their canon because the New Testament relates events it considers to be the fulfillment of Old Testament prophecies.

An enigma exists in Trinitarian Christianity regarding the oneness of the Father and the Son: if the two are actually one in spirit-essence, they cannot be separate, consubstantial spirit-essences. The Patripassionists put forth the logical sequitur to the belief in the unity of the Father's and the Son's spirit-essences: that it was actually the Father who was incarnated as a man and suffered on the cross. Since Patripassionism opposed the doctrine that only the Son suffered on the cross and that he offered his body as a sacrifice to the Father, it was condemned. But let us put aside the Patripassionists' valid objection that it is impossible for three consubstantial essences to be one essence and analyze whether the alleged consubstantiality of Jehovah's and Jesus' spirit-essences is actually consonant with the Bible and with good sense in general. I offer the following as evidence that, far from being consubstantial in spirit-essence with the great creator of the universe, Jesus was, as are all men to a greater or lesser degree, a "child of his place and time."

1. Jesus himself admitted his inferiority to the Holy Ghost. He said, "And whosoever speaketh a word against the son of man [Jesus] it shall be forgiven him: but whosoever speaketh against the Holy Ghost, it shall not be forgiven him, neither in this world, neither in the world to come" (Matthew 12:32).

2. The Fifth Commandment promulgated by Jehovah commands the Israelites to "Honor thy father and thy mother" (Exodus 20:12). Further, Jehovah says that a rebellious and disobedient son should be stoned to death (Deuteronomy 21:20-21). In Matthew 19:29 Jesus says, "And every one that hath forsaken houses, or brethren, or sisters,

or father, or mother, or wife, or children, or lands for my name's sake, shall receive a hundredfold, and shall inherit everlasting life." But how is it possible for one to honor his father and mother, as Jehovah commands, and yet forsake them for Jesus' name's sake? Jesus' confusion regarding the indissolubility of the bonds of marriage is revealed by his statement, "What therefore God hath joined together, let no man put asunder" (Matthew 19:6), which is diametrically opposed to his appeal to his listeners to forsake their wives for his name's sake. His general contempt for the ties of the blood is manifest in his attitude toward his mother, whom he addressed always as "woman," never as "mother." This can probably be attributed to the influence of the Essenes, a Jewish sect of that period. Scorning family life, in accordance with their teachings, he preached the exclusive fatherhood of God: "And call no man your father upon the earth; for one is your Father, which is in heaven" (Matthew 23:9) . Indeed, he regarded his disciples as being closer to him in spirit than his consanguinaries: "Who is my mother? and who are my brethren? And he stretched forth his hand toward his disciples, and said, Behold my mother and my Brethren!" (Matthew 12:48-49; Mark 3:34).

3. Jehovah allowed divorce without any reservations whatsoever. According to the twenty-fourth chapter of Deuteronomy, a husband was permitted to divorce his wife because of a "scandalous thing" he has found in her, no public explanation of his action being required. If the husband gave her a "bill of divorcement," she could legally remarry. There is no intimation in the Old Testament law that divorce was to be allowed because of "the hardness of your hearts" (Matthew 19:8), as Jesus put it. The law providing for the bill of divorcement was completely contrary to Jesus' moral precept that a divorced woman who remarried was committing adultery (Mark 10:12). Some maintain that Jesus' condemnation of divorce did not conflict with the Old Testa-

ment law which permitted it, for he explicitly sanctioned divorce in the case of adultery. But the fact that a Mosaic law permitted the divorced wife to remarry shows that the "scandalous thing" could not be adultery, for according to another Mosaic law, adulteresses were to be stoned to death, not given divorces. Contrary to Jesus' teachings, Deuteronomy 24:3-4 says that if a divorced woman who remarried was divorced by her second husband, she committed adultery if she went back to her first husband.

Further, Jesus ascribed the law of divorce to the indulgence of Moses, who in the Old Testament is nowhere presented as the formulator of any law, but only as an interlocutor transmitting the Law from God to the Israelites. Why did not Jesus say, "My Father allowed divorce because of the hardness of your hearts"? By saying, "Moses because of the hardness of your hearts suffered you to put away your wives: but from the beginning it was not so" (Matthew 19:8), he fraudulently absolved Jehovah of any complicity in the formulation of this law.

4. Jesus by implication disavowed any responsibility for either Jehovah or himself for the promulgation of the law "an eye for an eye and a tooth for a tooth," placing the blame for it on unknown persons of the past. This contradicts Chapter 24 of Leviticus, which clearly ascribes this law to Jehovah.

It is of interest to note that many Christians refer to "an eye for an eye and a tooth for a tooth" as "the old Jewish law of retribution." The fact is that there is no historical evidence that this law was ever implemented, either by the early Israelite tribes or by the Jewish nation, an offshoot of those early tribes, as a law of retribution. It was always interpreted as a law of compensation or restitution. "An eye for an eye . . ." was simply a metaphoric dictum for judicial proceedings in which equitable restitution or compensation was adjudicated to a plaintiff for damages incurred. Is it not a fact that this metaphoric principle is adhered to in all civilized countries, even those of Christendom? Jesus himself realized that this dictum was not a law of retribution but a metaphoric principle of legal action, for he gave the following example of a lawsuit to illustrate it: "And if any man will sue thee at the law, and take away thy coat, let him have thy cloak also" (Matthew 5:40).

5. Assuming Jesus and Jehovah are consubstantial in spirit-essence, it would appear that God, having promulgated a law for the stoning of harlots (Deuteronomy 22:21), later appeared on earth to circumvent its implementation without expressly abrogating it: "He that is without sin among you, let him first cast a stone at her" (John 8:7). Jesus seems to have implied that this law was unjust, for it granted to un-detected sinners the right to condemn a detected sinner. The question is: why would Jehovah, realizing this law to be un-just, hypocritical and uncharitable—and knowing that cen-turies later he would send one of his consubstantial spirit-essences in the person of Jesus to circumvent it—have pro-mulgated it at all?

6. There are instances in the New Testament narrative where Jesus shows ignorance and provincialism. For example, he did not speak fluent Hebrew; his dialect was a mixture of Hebrew and Aramaic. This reflects his northern, Galilean upbringing, in which Syrian influence was pronounced. The apology generally given by Christian theologians for Jesus' linguistic shortcomings is that Hebrew was not generally spoken at that time. The lie can be given to this claim from the text itself, for the Apostle Paul delivered a speech in Hebrew to a great throng in Jerusalem (Acts 21:40; 22:1-2). Could this have happened if Hebrew was not in wide use at that time?

7. When Jesus instructed his disciples to "Go teach all nations" (Matthew 28:19), why did he fail to inform them that America was across the ocean? Surely, if he were the

creator, he would have known of the great undiscovered continent and of the poor Indians who were in great ignorance of God and whose souls were in such desperate need of salvation! Is it not curious that for almost fifteen centuries after Jesus appeared on earth none of the "inspired men of God," including the popes, received any information from him about this great fact?

Although the Trinitarian Christians officially adhere to a belief in the spiritual consubstantiality of the three "persons" (monads) of the Triune God, they really think of the Father and the Son as being different spirit-substances. Their notion of disparity between the substances of the Father and the Son is certainly more consonant with the canonical Christian scriptures than the notion of the consubstantiality of these two essences, as I have shown. There is, therefore, a great self-contradiction within Trinitarian Christianity in that it alternately affirms and denies the spiritual consubstantiality of the Father and the Son.

When the Trinitarian Christian talks about the actions of "our Lord," he is almost always talking about what the Son of God did or said while he was joined with a human body on earth, never about anything either the Father or the Son did before the birth of that body. Indeed, it is only the entity Jesus—the compound of the Son and a human body— which the Trinitarian Christian thinks of as "our Lord." The preferential, possessive word "our" in "our Lord" probably indicates the Christian mind's reaction to the Jews' rejection of the doctrine of the human incarnation of God. The Jews' disbelief in the divinity of the monad joined with the body of Jesus has elicited in the antagonistic Christian mind a disposition to think of this entity as "*our* Lord," as though he were possessed—but only by those who believe in his divinity. The psychology involved in this feeling of possessiveness is actually the same as that of the ancient peoples who believed in antagonistic national patron gods.

47

The deeds and teachings of the entity Jesus are thus the Trinitarian Christian's principal theological interest. To him, the teachings of God from the mouth of Jesus seem more sublime than those promulgated by the Father, Jehovah. Indeed, more than one verse in the New Testament propounds this Christian belief. For example: "For the law was given by Moses [who got it from Jehovah], but grace and truth came by Jesus Christ" (John 1:17). Nay more, the teachings of Jesus are thought to have superseded much of the Old Testament law, despite the fact that Jesus is reported to have said, "For verily I say unto you, Till heaven and earth pass, one jot or one tittle shall in no wise pass from the law, till all be fulfilled" (Matthew 5:18).

To believe that the pronouncements God made when He was incarnate as a man are more important than those He made before He was joined with a man is as ridiculous as to believe the pronouncements President Johnson makes at the White House are necessarily inferior to those he makes at the Capitol. If God was teaching the Israelites through His interlocutors, the prophets, before He manifested Himself in the flesh as the entity Jesus, why should the words He spoke "in time" be considered more weighty than those He spoke "in eternity"? The dichotomy of the Bible into Old and New Testaments, as though the latter were superior to the former, is therefore inconsistent with the doctrine of Trinity.

While it is inconceivable that any Christian would not know the name of the human body with which the Son-monad was joined, many Christians do not think of the Father-monad's name as "Jehovah"; others think of the name "Jehovah" not as that of a real "person" of the Triune God-head but of the conceptual, "vengeful" god of the Jews.

Recently an organization of Roman Catholics called "Christ's Witnesses" was founded as a kind of parody to combat the growing influence of the non-Catholic, non-Trinitarian organization called "Jehovah's Witnesses." This illustrates that Trinitarian Christians really do not think of the words "Jehovah" and "Jesus" as being the names of a monad and an entity who are consubstantial in spirit-essence. The mental reflexes of the Trinitarian Christian, which should react the same way at the mention of either Jehovah or Jesus, are conditioned to react with greater reverence at the mention of the name "Jesus."

Perhaps the exalting of Jesus to a higher stature than Jehovah can be partially explained by Jesus' unselfish blood sacrifice, which Jehovah demanded in propitiation for the sins of the world. The average Christian thinks of Jehovah as stern and vengeful because He demanded a blood sacrifice to redeem man from Sin; on the other hand, he thinks of Jesus as the meek, submissive entity of the Son-monad, willingly complying with Jehovah's demand. It is only natural that his sympathy is with the sufferer. Thus, in the popular imagination the Father and the Son are actually rivals, not monads in perfect harmony.

The New Testament story of the voluntary sacrifice of an only son is derived from books written before the time of Jesus. A striking parallel can be seen in the Old Testament story of Abraham's willingness to sacrifice his son Isaac. A Freudian psychologist would probably think of this ancient story as expressing the parent's ambivalent and unconsciously destructive feelings toward his child.

Many other things in the New Testament are paralleled in the Old Testament. A few: the twelve tribes of Israel followed Jehovah through the desert and the twelve disciples followed Jesus; Elijah fasted for forty days in the desert and Moses was on Mount Sinai for forty days; also, Jesus fasted for forty days in the desert, and after his resurrection was on earth for forty days before his ascent to heaven. Indeed, forty seems to have been a magic number in the folklore of the Middle East, as illustrated by the story of Ali Baba and the forty thieves.

The Trinitarian Christians quote Jesus' statement "Before Abraham was, I am" (John 8:58) to support their belief that in his spirit-essence this entity was the Son-monad, existing coeternally with the Father-monad; but their splitting of history into B.C. (Before Christ) and A.D. (Anno Domini—the year of our Lord) illustrates that they think not of the Son-monad himself, but only of the Son-monad in combination with a human body, as being "our Lord."

But is it consonant with good sense that, if the entity Jesus intimated the existence of his spirit-essence from the beginning of time, he would have chosen the time of Abraham as an historical point of reference? For Adam, Eve, Noah, Cain, Abel, etc., also existed before Abraham. It would have been more informative and persuasive for Jesus to have said, "Before Adam was, I am." The probability is that he was talking not of chronological order, but of the order of importance.

The disparity in the length of time Christianity and Judaism have existed is symbolized by the relative ages of the protagonists who are believed to have founded them. Judaism may thus be called a Father religion; Christianity, a Son religion. Enigmatically, according to Trinitarianism the Father and the Son are coeternal, although the entire notion of a father-son relationship is one involving a difference in age between two monads so related, indeed of the siring of one by the other.

Since Jesus died, was resurrected and ascended to heaven before reaching the age of thirty-five, his body is thought of as remaining eternally young. Indeed, this is probably the psychological reason why the monad which was joined with the body of Jesus is called the Son, despite its eternal coexistence with the other monads of the Triune Godhead.

It has been nineteen centuries since the entity Jesus ascended to heaven, but Christian artists have always depicted him either as a child or a young man on earth—never as he is, sitting at the right hand of the Father.

In the New Testament, Jesus is called, among other things, "the Lord": "And he [Paul] said, Who art thou Lord? And the Lord said, I am Jesus whom thou persecutest" (Acts 9:5). In addition to being called "the Lord," Jesus is also called "our Lord" (Romans 1:3). Like Jesus, God in the New Testament is referred to as "the Lord": "For Moses truly said unto the fathers, a prophet shall the Lord your God raise up unto you of your brethren" (Acts 3:22). Therefore, the Trinitarian Christians believe the words "Jesus," "the Lord" and "God," wherever they occur in the New Testament, are designations of God, although the name "Jesus" also connotes the human entity of which one of the three God-monads is a component. According to the doctrine of Trinity, they should believe that any of these words, wherever they appear in the New Testament, refer to either the same monad or a consubstantial monad to which the words "the Lord" and "God" refer wherever they appear in the Old Testament.

Again, in all Trinitarian Christian English language versions of the Old Testament, the appellative "the Lord" is substituted for the proper name transliterated "Jehovah." Also, in foreign language Trinitarian Christian versions of the Old Testament, such as Luther's German version, an appellative meaning "the Lord" appears wherever the name "Jehovah" is found in the original Hebrew. And in English language versions of the Old Testament made by Jewish scholars one finds the same anomaly.

Now the Greek Septuagint version of the Old Testament was composed by Jewish scholars in the second century B.C.E. In the fourth century, C.E., St. Jerome used the Greek Septuagint version of the Old Testament then extant and the Greek language New Testament writings to render the Bible into his Latin Vulgate. All subsequent Trinitarian Christian versions of the Bible were derived from the Latin Vulgate. The English language versions of the Old Testament composed by Jewish scholars are of relatively recent vintage. These scholars made use of the many existing Trinitarian Christian versions as well as the original Hebrew text and extant editions of the Greek Septuagint. In the Latin Vulgate, wherever the name "Jehovah" should appear, one finds the word "Dominus," the Latin appellative meaning "the lord." Some believe that in the original Greek Septuagint, a Greek transliteration of the name "Jehovah" appeared wherever this name appeared in the Hebrew text. But it was revised many times by Trinitarian Christians before Jerome translated it into Latin. It is probable that these revisers, thinking that a proper name of the Lord other than "Jesus" was inimical to Church unity, substituted the appellative "Kyrios," meaning "the Lord," wherever the transliterated name "Jehovah" appeared; and that later Jerome, using a revised version, unwittingly used this appellative instead of the name "Jehovah."

It is evident that the words "the Lord" have always been used by monotheists as an appellative for God. As I have pointed out, the ancient Phoenicians used the word transliterated as "Baal," meaning "the Lord," to designate God. But the Israelites who were contemporaries of the Phoenicians and were polytheists used the word "Jehovah" to name their patron god. And it was only after the Babylonian Exile, during which the Jews as a nation were won over to monotheism, that they came to think of the name "Jehovah" as being that of the Lord. The substitution of the appellative "the Lord" for the name "Jehovah" in those books of the Bible composed prior to the Babylonian Exile therefore represents a gross distortion of the original writers' thought.

At any rate, wherever the words "the Lord" appear in both the Old and the New Testament, they are interpreted by

Trinitarian Christian theologians as an appellative of God. But the Jews do not accept the New Testament as being a revelation from God. And since the words "Jesus Christ" do not appear in the Old Testament, and the moral precepts imputed to "the Lord" by the Old Testament are in many instances at variance with those imputed to "Jesus Christ," "the Lord," or "God" by the New Testament, the confused Trinitarian Christians feel impelled to interpret parts of the Old Testament as primitive tribes' perverse imaginings of God. But if one reads the Bible honestly, he will find in the New Testament the notion of everlasting punishment for the unrepentant sinner, with no opportunity for parole or reprieve once judgment has been passed against him; however, nowhere in the Old Testament books of the Law will he find the notion that the Lord punishes unrepentant sinners with everlasting punishment. Often the punishments imputed to the Lord in the Old Testament are of a corrective nature designed to bring the sinner back to the straight path.

Thus, the Trinitarian Christian theologians find themselves in this quandary: having canonized both Old and New Testaments, they are on the one hand obliged to uphold the consistency of the substance of "the Lord" not only within each book alone, but in both books considered as one work; at the same time, they feel impelled to denigrate parts of the Old Testament.

The truth is that the substance of "the Lord," as delineated in each Testament itself is inconsistent. How then can the two Testaments be consistent with each other? If, then, we believe—as we must if we are monotheists—that God does not change and that He is infinitely superior to man, we must concede that spurious attributes are imputed to Him in all extant versions of the Bible.

Chapter 3

THE MESSIAH

The Trinitarian Christian theologians claim that the Messiah and one of the three "persons" of the Triune God are actually one and the same monad and that ever since the time of Moses the Jews have been expecting God to appear on earth as a man called the Messiah. The truth is that the Jews have never thought of the Messiah-monad and the Son of God as being the same monad. Nor is the Christian doctrine of redemption through the shed blood of the Messiah predicated on the fulfillment of Old Testament prophecies, but on their distortion and adulteration.

It should be understood that the meaning of the word "Messiah" has changed drastically through the centuries. The belief in the existence of a special agent of God called the Messiah did not germinate in the Israelite psyche until long after the age in which Moses allegedly lived (*c.* 1500-1400 B.C.E.); this belief has no connection with the formative precepts of the faith of Israel, which are delineated fully in the Pentateuch. Indeed, the word "Messiah" itself does not appear in these books.

How did the word "Messiah" originate and what was its earliest significance? It was evidently neologistic when Saul was elevated, through the ceremony of anointment, to the throne of Israel in the eleventh century B.C.E. This ceremony signified the investiture of divine election: "And Samuel took a flask of oil, and poured it upon his [Saul's] head, and kissed him, and said, Behold it is because the Lord hath anointed thee over his inheritance as chief" (1 Samuel 10:1). The word "Messiah" is simply the English transliteration of the Hebrew word for "anointed one," which was used for the first time by the Israelites as a title for their first king, Saul. The Greek word for "anointed one" is "Christ": "We have found the Messias, which is being interpreted, the Christ" (John 1:41). According to Exodus 30:25-31, the Aaronite priests were consecrated by anointment with "holy oil." But the title "anointed one" [1] was evidently withheld until the days of the Israelite kings. That Saul in his day was called the Messiah is evident from several passages in the two books of Samuel. For example, in his famous eulogy in honor of the slain Saul, David calls him the "anointed [one] of the Lord" (2 Samuel 1:14). It is thus clear that the word "Messiah" was originally the title of the King of Israel, a temporal office which was, moreover, occupied successively by various individuals.

The reign of David, who succeeded Saul on being anointed King (see 1 Chronicles 14:8), ushered in an epoch which lasted until the start of the Babylonian Exile (*c.* 582 B.C.E.). All the kings of Judah who reigned during this epoch of five centuries are alleged to have been of Davidic descent. From the scriptural narrative, it can be deduced that the passing of the title "Messiah" to the heir-apparent was automatic on the death of the incumbent king, and that the repetition of the ceremony of anointment was considered superfluous, except when the heir-apparent was deposed by a younger brother, as was the case when Solomon took the throne from Adonijah. The struggle between Solomon and Adonijah, sons of David, resulted in the split of the country into the Kingdom of the North, called "the Kingdom of

[1] In Hebrew, this substantive, titular construction is derived from the participial "anointed" which appears in Leviticus 4:5.

Samaria" or simply "Israel," and the Kingdom of the South, called "Judah."

The portion of the Bible which narrates events subsequent to the schism was evidently written by partisans of Judah. The kings of Judah were all descended from David; the kings of Samaria, of whom Jeroboam, the son of Nebat, was the first, were not. Thus the messianic title passed in turn to each of the kings of Judah, but not to the kings of Samaria.

There can be little doubt that the title "The Messiah, the son of David" dates from the five-century epoch of the reign of the House of David over the Kingdom of Judah. The ancient people of Judah thought of the word "Messiah" not as the title of one and only one monad in eternity, but rather of one and only one monad at a particular time; each succeeding king of Judah was called the Messiah during his incumbency as king. The Davidic line of succession to the throne of Judah was finally terminated by the Babylonian Exile.

Before analyzing the contribution that the canonical Hebrew prophets (eighth century B.C.E.—fifth century B.C.E.) unknowingly made to the evolution of messianism, it is important to note that Isaiah, the son of Amoz, who lived in the eighth century B.C.E. during the successive reigns of Kings Uzziah, Jotham, Ahaz and Hezekiah (Isaiah 1:1), could not possibly have known about Cyrus (Isaiah 45:1) and the Babylonian Exile (sixth century B.C.E.). Therefore, as has been said, the Book of Isaiah is a combination of the works of at least two men, one of whom lived during the Babylonian Exile—Isaiah, the son of Amoz, being generally called Isaiah I; the Babylonian Isaiah, Deutero-Isaiah.

Through a misinterpretation of the pre-Exilic Isaiah I's vision of "the end of days . . . when nations shall beat their swords into plough-shares" (Isaiah 2:2-4), the title "Messiah" eventually came to acquire the mysterious eschatological significance which is attached to it in Jewish and Christian

56

theology to this day. It is impossible that Isaiah I correlated the marvelous events he envisioned with the appearance on earth of a unique monad who would thereafter throughout all eternity alone be called the Messiah. He lived in an era of four temporal Davidic kings, each of whom was called the Messiah. Therefore, there could have been no messianic expectation in his day. The prophet Micah, a contemporary of Isaiah I, in language identical with the latter's prophecy of the "end of days," prophesies: "And in the end of days it shall come to pass, that the mountain of the Lord's house shall be established on the top of the mountains, and shall be exalted above the hills: and unto it shall people flow" (Micah 4:1). Like Isaiah I, Micah does not correlate the events of the "end of days" with the appearance of a descendant of David who would thereafter be the Messiah forever.

It was natural for the Jewish exiles in Babylon to search the prophetic writings for something from which they could derive hope and comfort. At this critical juncture in Jewish history occurred the semantic metamorphosis by which a title, until then of only temporal significance, was transformed to mean a king of the House of David who, after the return of the Jews from exile, was to rule in Jerusalem forever. Ezekiel (*c.* 620-570 B.C.E.), a prophet of the Babylonian Exile, interpreted the vision of the "end of days" of Isaiah I and Micah as being the glorious aftermath of the Exilic nightmare. He thought David himself would return to rule forever in Jerusalem: "And I will appoint over them one shepherd, and he shall feed them, namely My servant David: he it is that shall feed them, and he it is that shall be unto them for a shepherd" (Ezekiel 34:23); "And My servant David shall be king over them; and they all shall have one shepherd . . . and David my servant shall be prince unto them forever" (Ezekiel 37:24-25) .

Evidently the Jews in Babylon acquired from the Babylonians a doctrine which prior to that time had not been a precept of their faith—the resurrection of the dead. They correlated the coming establishment of the messianic kingdom at the "end of days" after the exile with a general resurrection of the dead: "And many of them that sleep in the dust of the earth shall awake, some to everlasting life, and some to reproaches and everlasting abhorrence" (Daniel 12:2).

Although Ezekiel's prophecy of David's resurrection and return as the "one shepherd" is not a favorite quotation of the Christians (they believe that Jesus, not David, is the one shepherd), it is Ezekiel's notion of the "one shepherd" who "shall be prince over them forever" which is undeniably the Biblical foundation of what people call messianism; for whatever the difference between Christian and Jewish messianism, the one thing they have in common is the notion of "one shepherd."

None of the prophets I have mentioned actually used the word "Messiah." But since Ezekiel, the father of messianism, said that David (the progenitive Messiah of all Messiahs succeeding him) was expected to return as the "one shepherd," this explains the genesis of the phrase "the messianic expectation," for people for centuries have been saying, "The Messiah is coming."

When the exiles returned to Palestine (c. 587 B.C.E.), David did not return from the dead, as Ezekiel had predicted. As a result, a drastic innovation was introduced into messianism. Cyrus the Great, who had defeated the Babylonians and returned the Jews to their homeland, was invested by Deutero-Isaiah with the title "Messiah": "Thus hath said the Lord to his anointed [one], to Cyrus, whose right hand I have holden to subdue nations before him" (Isaiah 45:1). Although David failed to return, the hope for a great savior remained deeply ingrained in the minds of the people; the words "The

Messiah is coming," which had been on the tongues of all Jews, thus were no longer thought of as necessarily signifying the coming appearance of David, but of any great deliverer. Thus, it came about that Cyrus, who was certainly not of the House of David, nor even a Jew, came to be invested with the title "Messiah." But as Cyrus proved to be as mortal as anyone else, the myth that he was the Messiah, the "one shepherd" who was to rule forever, was eventually discredited.

Since the death of Cyrus, there has been no unanimity of opinion among the Jews as to who and what the Messiah will be. The one notion in which all devout Jews agree is that his appearance will signal the "end of days." That this belief has held sway among Jews is evident from the New Testament. When John the Baptist was proclaiming that the Messiah was soon to come, he said, "Repent ye; for the kingdom of heaven is at hand" (Matthew 3:2). In Jewish messianism "the kingdom of heaven" is the state of bliss which will exist on earth at "the end of days."

Cyrus, however, was by no means the last Gentile to be endowed by Jews with the title "Messiah." In the sixteenth century, for example, when early in his career as a Protestant, Luther espoused the cause of the Jews, many thought him the Messiah. This delusion was later shattered when he tried and failed to convert the Jews to Christianity and consequently turned violently against them.

A statement imputed to Hillel (first century B.C.E.) reads: "Israel need not expect any Messiah, for they had him already in the days of Hezekiah" (724-696 B.C.E.). This sage thus realized that the messianic hope, under the pressure of continual disappointment, had become blurred; and he feared divisiveness would result from the inevitable manifold interpretations. Later the Christians inherited this blurred image of the messianic hope, made further innovations, and

59

multiplied the confusion tenfold by the injection of the "suffering savior" notion, which is totally incompatible with Jewish messianism.

Malachi (fifth century B.C.E.), the last of the prophets whose writings have been canonized by the Jews, says nothing about the Messiah. He simply predicted that Elijah, who had lived many centuries before, was to be the precursor of the "coming of the great and dreadful day of the Lord" (Malachi 3:1, 23). Although in these verses there is no reference to the Messiah, many interpret their words as a prophecy that Elijah would be the precursor of the Messiah. According to the New Testament, Jesus, thinking himself the Messiah, quoted Malachi's prophecy, then asserted that John the Baptist was Elijah (Matthew 17:12-13; Luke 7:27-28). This suggests Jesus believed in reincarnation. John the Baptist could not have been the resurrected Elijah, for his parents were Elizabeth and Zacharias (Luke, 1). The only way the monad which had been a component of the entity Elijah could have later become a component of the entity John the Baptist was through reincarnation. Significantly, John the Baptist, asked if he was Elijah, denied it (see John 1:21).

Just as the Jews through assimilating Babylonian beliefs came to believe in the resurrection of the dead, in the ensuing period they were greatly influenced by the Iranian conquerors of Babylon. Many sects which arose under the influence of Iranian teachings expounded a belief in the immortality of the soul: it leaves the body immediately after death to receive either eternal reward in paradise or eternal punishment in hell. The notion of the immortality of the soul is quite different from the notion of the resurrection of the dead; the doctrine of the latter is that the soul slumbers while the body is dead and is revived when the body is resurrected. The new belief in the immortality of the soul was completely contrary to Biblical teaching: "For the living know that they will die; but the dead know nothing at all,

nor have they longer any reward; for their memory is for-
gotten" (Ecclesiastes 9:5); "The dead praise not the Lord,
neither any that go down into silence" (Psalms 115:17); "For
in death men do not remember Thee: in the nether world,
who shall give Thee thanks?" (Psalms 6:6).

Nevertheless, the new doctrine gained thousands of adherents through the harsh impetus of the Hellenist and Roman
occupations of Palestine which followed the Iranian period.

To the present day, paradise is called "The Garden of
Eden" in orthodox Judaism. But it is difficult to understand
how the Garden of Eden, which the Bible locates in the
Tigris-Euphrates valley—a definite terrestrial locale—can be
the scene of a community of disembodied souls.

For well over two thousand years Judaism has contained
a paradox, teaching the existence of both paradise and the
messianic kingdom on earth at the "end of days." If departed
souls are already being rewarded in paradise and if all deserving people of the present and future will be so rewarded when they die, what need is there for the dead to be
resurrected in a messianic kingdom on earth at the "end of
days"?

The New Testament strongly reflects this paradox in
Judaism. It alternately propounds the "resurrection of the
dead" (John 5:28-29), which involves the temporary decease
of the soul, and "everlasting life" (John 4:14). The two
incompatible doctrines are even intertwined in one sentence: "And this is the will of him that sent me, that every
one which seeth the son, and believeth in him, may have
everlasting life; and I will raise him up at the last day"
(John 6:40). In order to harmonize these doctrines, Christian
thinkers have devised the argument that the soul, being
indeed immortal, leaves the body when it dies, to be reunited with it at the time of the general resurrection of the
dead. However, the conciliation of the two doctrines precipi-
tates a quandary of double jeopardy: one judgment occurs

61

immediately after death, the soul receiving its reward, temporary expurgation, or damnation; the other judgment occurs after the soul is reunited with its resurrected body. This problem of double jeopardy remains a thorn in the side of Christian theologians.

The renunciation of this materialistic life on earth and the expectation of reward in either the coming messianic kingdom on earth or the paradise of departed souls seems to have been the prevailing religious atmosphere in which the mind of Jesus was conditioned. Deterministic maxims such as "The powers that be are ordained of God" (Romans 13:1) were used by the collaborationist Jewish clergy who were in the pay of the Roman army of occupation in order to promote and sanctify popular subservence to Roman rule. Significantly, Jesus himself at no time inveighed against the Roman occupation. On the contrary, he actually upheld Caesar's right to oppress and exploit the Holy Land. "Render therefore unto Caesar the things which are Caesar's and unto God the things that are God's" (Matthew 22:21) was his impotent and evasive retort to the Pharisees' pointed question about Roman taxation. One is tempted to inquire of Trinitarian Christians, who are supposed to believe that Jesus was not only the Messiah but also a human incarnation of God Himself, whether it was consistent for God to collaborate with a Gentile enemy when He himself promised Canaan to the seed of Abraham as an "everlasting possession" (Genesis 17:18; 48:4), and was able to "cast out many nations before thee . . . even nations mightier than thou" (Deuteronomy 7:1-8). What, indeed, would the American colonists have thought of Washington had he said, when faced with the question of taxation without representation, "Render unto King George the things that are of King George and render unto God the things that are of God"?

Much of the confusion of the Christians can be traced to their peculiar exegesis regarding certain Old Testament statements and prophecies pertaining to several Messiahs and non-Messiahs which holds that all these statements and prophecies refer to one entity: Jesus.

For example, the Christian clergy claim that the birth of Jesus from a virgin was prophesied by Isaiah: "Therefore the Lord Himself shall give you a sign: Behold a virgin shall conceive, and bear a son, and shall call his name Immanuel" (Isaiah 7:14). The Hebrew word *"ha-almah,"* which means "this young woman," is here translated "a virgin" to suit the convenience of Christian delusion. The claim is also made that the name "Immanuel," which means "God is with us," is a reference to the divinity of Jesus.

As this Old Testament verse, which is so cherished by the Trinitarian Christians, is usually quoted out of context, let me clarify its meaning by quoting also the verses that follow immediately: "Therefore the Lord Himself shall give you a sign: behold a virgin shall conceive, and bear a son, and shall call his name Immanuel. Curd and honey shall he eat, when he knoweth to refuse the evil, and choose the good. Yea, before the child shall know to refuse the evil, and choose the good, the land whose two kings thou hast a horror of shall be forsaken of both her kings" (Isaiah 7:14-16). If we read the whole chapter, we cannot doubt that Isaiah I was talking about contemporary events (eighth century B.C.E.). The first verse of the chapter tells of the impending attack on Jerusalem by Rezin, King of Syria, and by Pekah, King of Samaria. The Lord then enjoins Isaiah to calm the apprehensions of Ahaz, King of Judah, by promising a "sign" which would augur the raising of the siege of Jerusalem, and the destruction of its two adversaries through the intervention of another king on the side of Judah. "This young woman" was, no doubt, Isaiah's wife. Isaiah was in the habit of giving his sons symbolic names such as Maher-Shalal-hash-bas (Speedy booty, sudden spoil) and Shear-Yashub (a remnant shall return). He thought of the birth of his children as signs: "Behold, I and the children whom the Lord hath given me are for signs and for tokens in Israel" (8:18).

Besides Immanuel there are other Old Testament names which designate persons, yet refer to God. For example: Elimelech (God is my king), Elihu (He is my God), Eliab (God is my father). Are all these people deities because reference to God is made in their names? Furthermore, was Jesus ever called Immanuel either by his mother or by any of his contemporaries? Is it possible that Jesus, if he really was God, would not "know to refuse the evil, and choose the good"? And was Jesus an eater of "curd and honey"? By all accounts, he was a flesh eater.

For the moment, let us waive all these objections. Let us assume "Immanuel" to be a reference to Jesus; the word *"ha-almah"* as meaning a virgin; the word *"ha-almah"* as used by Isaiah as referring specifically to the Virgin Mary; and the "sign" of a virgin conceiving a child as indicating the birth of the Messiah.

A sign is a physical indication or directive which may be perceived only through one or more of the five senses. For example: if the skies are blue, it is a sign that no rain is in the offing in the immediate future. Another example: smoke is a sign of fire. But can conception by a virgin be perceived by any of the five senses? Could the neighbors of the Virgin Mary perceive this "sign"? Apart from Mary, the only persons who could have perceived this "sign" were medical doctors who may have examined her.

The explanation offered by some Christians is that the prophecy of the "sign" was not addressed to those who were to be aware of the circumstances of Jesus' birth at the time it occurred, but to those who were to become aware of his messiahship during the course of his three-year ministry. These Christians contend that those who witnessed the miracles of Jesus and heard him speak should have deduced he was the Messiah and should have realized therefore that

64

he was born of a virgin in fulfillment of Isaiah's prophecy of the "sign."

This argument can be refuted in the following manner: Suppose you were driving a car on a highway and passed a speed-limit sign which happened to be covered. Would it be judicious for an officer to write you a ticket for exceeding the speed limit indicated by the sign which was not visible? Of course, having received the ticket, you would deduce, in retrospect, that the covered sign you passed indicated such-and-such a speed limit. Likewise, the "sign" of a virgin conceiving a child is certainly a sign which is covered. But of what value is a sign if it is covered? Instead of the virgin's conceiving indicating the Messiah's birth, the realization by those who knew him in his adulthood of his exalted function was to reveal to them, in retrospect, his mother's virginity. This is a theological placing of the cart before the horse, and inverts the whole purpose of signs.

It is also of the greatest importance to point out that, according to the Gospels, Jesus refused to resort to signs to relieve the unbelieving of their doubts. In response to the Pharisees' request that he show them a sign, he declared: "An evil and adulterous generation seeketh after a sign; and there shall no sign be given it, but the sign of the prophet Jonas: For as Jonas was three days and three nights in the whale's belly, so shall the son of man be three days and three nights in the heart of the earth" (Matthew 12:39-40). This declaration is at variance with the many instances of miracles the Gospels credit to Jesus, as well as with the Trinitarian Christian claim that Jesus proved he was God by performing miracles. If it is true that he performed miracles, then by his own words he was catering to the craving for signs of a "wicked and adulterous generation." Moreover, was Jesus "three days and three nights in the heart of the earth"? According to Christian belief, he was crucified on a Friday afternoon, and rose from the dead the following Sunday morning. Therefore, he was in the heart of the earth less than two days and two nights.

Let us take another example of an Old Testament verse quoted out of context in the New Testament: "But thou Bethlehem . . . out of thee shall one come forth unto Me that is to be a ruler in Israel" (Micah 5:1). The writer of Matthew 2:6, quoting this verse, claims it presages Jesus' birth in Bethlehem. Reading the fifth chapter of Micah in a fuller context, one finds: "But thou Bethlehem . . . out of thee shall one come forth unto Me that is to be ruler in Israel . . . and this man shall be the peace, when the Assyrian shall come into our land, and when he treadeth within our borders" (Micah 5:1-6). There can be no question whom the prophet was referring to. Although he did not mention the name of this particular Messiah, it is revealed by the contemporaneous writings of Isaiah I: "Then came the word of the Lord to Isaiah saying, Go, and say to Hezekiah, thus saith the Lord . . . I will deliver thee and this city out of the hand of the king of Assyria" (Isaiah 38:4-6). There are also accounts of this siege of Jerusalem (*c*. 711 B.C.E.) by Sennacherib, King of Assyria, and its deliverance by Hezekiah, in 2 Kings, Chapters 18-20, as well as in 2 Chronicles, Chapter 32. How could Micah's prophecy conceivably refer to the entity called Jesus in the New Testament? The Assyrian Kingdom was extirpated in the sixth century before his birth. And the words "*a* ruler" imply that he was to be merely a temporal sovereign, not the everlasting ruler one could infer from this verse had the writer written "*the* ruler." Furthermore, Jesus denied being either a ruler or the ruler in Israel, stating, "My Kingdom is not of this world" (John 18:36).

Correlating the twentieth chapter of the Second Book of Kings with the fifty-third chapter of Isaiah, one sees that it was Hezekiah, not Jesus, who was "a man of pains and acquainted with disease" (Isaiah 53:3); and it was Hezekiah,

66

not Jesus, who was "smitten of God and afflicted. But he was wounded for our transgressions" (53:5). The so-called prophecies of the fifty-third chapter of Isaiah are all written in the past tense. If Isaiah were prophesying here, would he use the past tense?

It was also Hezekiah whose days were prolonged for fifteen years (2 Kings 20:6) after he was "sick unto death" (20:1). If the reader checks the last reference, let him note this interesting parallel: Hezekiah, having been "sick unto death," going to the house of the Lord on the third day after his healing (2 Kings 20:5) and Jesus going to the Father on the third day after his crucifixion.

Christian theologians even go so far as to claim that the appellative "the prince of peace" in Isaiah 9:5 is one of the names of Jesus. This appellative does not appear anywhere in the New Testament. Isaiah 9:5 should properly read: "For a child is born unto us, a son hath been given unto us, and the government is placed on his shoulders: and his name is called wonderful, counsellor of the mighty God, of the everlasting Father, the prince of peace." "Counsellor of the mighty God" is erroneously rendered by Trinitarian Christians: "Counsellor, the mighty God." No doubt, Isaiah meant Hezekiah by his words "the prince of peace," for we find the words "Behold, for peace I had great bitterness" in Hezekiah's poem in the thirty-eighth chapter of Isaiah; and Micah, speaking of Hezekiah, wrote, "This man shall be the peace" (Micah 5:4). Moreover, by implication Jesus disavowed for himself the appellative "the prince of peace" by his declamation: "I come not to bring peace but a sword" (Matthew 10:34).

Matthew 2:15 says that King Herod sought to kill Jesus, for which reason Mary fled with him to Egypt: "that it might be fulfilled which was spoken of the Lord by the prophet, saying, out of Egypt have I called My son." This is another example of the out of context quotation. It is taken from

Hosea 1:11:

> When Israel was a child, then
> I loved him,
> And out of Egypt I called My son.

In the first place this verse is not even a prophecy, for it relates an event which happened prior to its composition; secondly, it is evident that "My son" is the nation Israel, not Jesus.

One of the verses Roman Catholic theologians have quoted out of context to demonstrate that events in the New Testament were prophesied in the Old Testament is Genesis 3:15: "And I will put enmity between thee [the serpent] and the woman, and between thy seed and her seed; they shall bruise thy head, and thou shalt bruise their heel." The "serpent," "the woman," and "her seed" are alleged to be allegorical references to Satan, the Virgin Mary and Jesus respectively. How then do these theologians explain the sentence immediately following it in the text: "Unto the woman he said: I will greatly multiply thy pain and thy travail, in pain shalt thou bring forth children"? (Genesis 3:16.) Those who believe that "the woman" refers to the Virgin Mary must concede that according to these verses she was to have more than one child, for "the woman . . . shalt bring forth *children*." The dogma of the perpetual virginity of Mary precludes the possibility of such a concession by Roman Catholic theologians. It is plain that "the woman" of the third chapter of Genesis is Eve, archetype of womanhood, suffering pain in childbirth; that the "seed of the woman" is mankind; and that "the serpent" is the general species of crawling reptile, whose head is continually bruised by the human heel.

Let me give another example of Christian chicanery. They cite as a prophecy referring to Jesus 2 Samuel 7:12-13: "When thy days are fulfilled, and thou shalt sleep with thy fathers, I will set up thy seed after thee, that shall proceed out of thy body, and I will establish his kingdom. He shall build a house for My name, and I will establish the throne of his kingdom for ever." The Lord is here talking to David through the prophet Nathan. He is obviously talking about Solomon, for it is Solomon who will build the temple in Jerusalem. Verse 14, "I will be to him a father and he shall be to Me a son; if he commit iniquity, I will chasten him with the rod of men," states clearly that this particular Messiah was to be punished for his own sins, not for the sins of the world, the vicarious punishment the Christians believe the Messiah was predestined to suffer.

The great fraud of that kind of Old Testament exegesis which claims that certain of its prophecies, such as the ones I have just cited, pertain to the Man of Nazareth is that these prophecies really pertain to persons who lived many centuries before the Christian era.

The New Testament contains a phantasmagoria of Jewish messianism and non-Jewish mythology. This is manifest in the various names, pseudonyms and titles which it applies to Jesus: high priest; prophet; lamb; son of man; son of David; judge; savior; Immanuel; minister to the circumcision; Christ.

Did Jesus always think of himself as being the Messiah (Christ)? The evidence is that early in his ministry he had misgivings about it. From the question "Whom do ye say that I am?" (Matthew 16:15) which he put to his disciples, it can be inferred that at the time he had not apprised even his immediate followers of his feeling that he might be the Messiah. Probably he was putting out feelers and soliciting encouragement. Peter's reply, "Thou art the Christ, the son of the living God" (Matthew 16:16), seems to have relieved Jesus' doubts. Nevertheless, his admonition, "Tell no man I am the Christ" (Matthew 16:20), indicates he was not absolutely sure of being the Messiah, and outside of his small circle of followers wished to remain "incognito" in this respect. Kierkegaard called Jesus "The Great Incognito." Even assuming Jesus was the Messiah, since he did not wish to be publicly known in this role, he cannot justly be called a "rejected Messiah." This is one of the incongruities of Christian thinking.

With regard to the appellative "the son of God," it should be understood that during Paul's ministry this combination of words was thought of only as being a title; it had not yet come to be interpreted in the Trinitarian sense as implying the divinity of its bearer. There are many passages in both Testaments which indicate that the title "Son of God" did not symbolize divinity in the minds of the authors, as shown by the following: "The sons of God came to present themselves before the Lord" (Job 1:6); "Ye are the children of the Lord your God" (Deuteronomy 14:1) ; "For as many as are led by the spirit of God, they are the sons of God" (Romans 8:14).

Jesus himself was not a Trinitarian, as shown by the following: "And behold, one came and said unto him, Good Master, what good things shall I do, that I may have eternal life? And he said unto him, Why callest thou me good? There is none good but one, that is God: but if thou wilt enter into life, keep the commandments" (Matthew 19:16-17). However, the Roman Catholic Douay version reads: "Why dost thou ask me about what is good?" The Roman Catholic version thus avoids the implication that Jesus did not consider himself good. But Jesus, who called himself "the son of God," among other things, could not have implied by this appellative that he was one of the three "persons" of the Godhead, for he also said, "My Father is greater than I" (John 14:28). "I and my Father are one" (John 10:30) is one of the passages Trinitarian Christians cite to prove that Jesus claimed he was one of the three persons of the Godhead. Jesus prayed that his disciples would also be one with God (see John 17:21). If being *one* with God is tantamount to *being* God, we reach the absurd conclusion that the disciples were potentially also part of the Godhead.

The Apostle Paul, who was not one of the disciples who knew Jesus face to face, was the first Christian to break completely with the Jewish religion. According to the Book of the Acts of the Apostles, Paul preached only to the Jews in the period immediately following his so-called conversion to Christ, but later turned to the Gentiles. Acts 13:46 quotes Paul as saying to the Jews: "It was necessary that the word of God should first have been spoken to you: but seeing ye put it from you, and judge yourselves unworthy of everlasting life, lo, we turn to the Gentiles." Evidently Paul was ignorant of Jesus' warning to his disciples to "go not unto the way of the Gentiles . . . but go rather to the lost sheep of the house of Israel" (Matthew 10:6). Thus the founding of universal Christianity was brought about not by the teachings that Jesus promulgated during his earthly ministry, but because of Paul's exasperation with the Jewish multitudes. Could it have been the case that Paul, believing himself the vicegerent of Jesus, thought of his own persecution by Jews as being tantamount to the persecution of Jesus himself? And that *he* originated the notion that the Jews "rejected Christ"?

That Paul was deluded in his belief that he was Jesus' vicegerent is revealed by his ingenuous statement, "I am a Pharisee" (Acts 23:6). Evidently he was completely unaware of Jesus' animadversions against the Pharisee sect. Paul's "conversion" on the road to Damascus, at which time he thought he saw and heard Jesus, was probably caused by one of those mirages so commonly experienced in Middle Eastern deserts.

The Roman Catholic clergy, who became the leaders of the loosely federated feudal society of Western Europe, found

71

the New Testament phrase "good works" to be of great value in the implementation of their historic role in Europe. "Faith without works is dead" (James 2:17) is one of the few quotations from the New Testament every Roman Catholic is certain to know; and to the Catholic mind, the salvation of one's soul is contingent even more upon the performance of "good works" than on the mental exercise of faith.

In the Roman Catholic system, the monad which was joined with the body of Jesus is the second "person" of the Triune Godhead—the Son of God; Jesus is also the Messiah.

The Roman Catholics believe that Jesus will be the Judge of the resurrected dead, as expressed in the Requiem Mass:

> Day of anger, day of mourning,
> When to ashes all is burning,
> Seer and Sibyl gave the warning,
> O what fear man's bosom rendeth,
> When from Heaven the Judge descendeth,
> On whose sentence all dependeth.

The Roman Catholic clergy can cite New Testament passages to corroborate this. For example: "For the Father judgeth no man, but hath committed all judgment to the son" (John 5:22). Needless to say, the contrary doctrine that Jesus is not a judge can also be found in this most confused of books: "Ye judge after the flesh; I judge no man" (John 8:15). The inanity of Roman Catholic theology is evident in the above imputation to the Messiah of functions which in effect reveal him to be a split personality—both savior and condemner.

Again, the Roman Catholic clergy were forced to incorporate into their canon the Old Testament as well as the New because the latter relates events it alleges were the fulfillment of Old Testament prophecies. The Church fathers had to resort to chicanery in order to establish an intricate

72

concatenation between the two Testaments, which in many ways are doctrinally disparate. Regarding the Messiah, their syllogistic reasoning ran: Is it not true that the Old Testament contains references to the Messiah? Since we know Jesus is the Messiah, there can be no doubt the writers of the Old Testament were writing about Jesus when they referred to the Messiah. It would be just as sensible for someone to say the framers of the Constitution had Johnson in mind when they wrote about the President.

The Protestants, on the other hand, have chosen to play their own tunes on the New Testament fiddle. For this book contains such a conglomeration of inconsistent and contradictory doctrine that it has come to mean all things to all men. The Protestants believe, as do the Catholics, that the protagonist of the New Testament was the entity whom God titled "Messiah." But the aim of the Protestant reformers was to lure people from the Catholic Church by setting up a rival church which denied that one's salvation is conditional upon his performance of "good works." John Calvin, the chief doctrinal protagonist of the Reformation, made his place in history by disparaging the Catholic doctrine of "good works." He taught that the Messiah, caring nothing for "good works," rewards the believer with a place in heaven simply for his belief, and punishes the unbeliever by sending him to hell simply for his unbelief. These were some of Calvin's favorite quotations: "For by grace are ye saved through faith; and that not of yourself: it is the gift of God" (Ephesians 2:8) ; "By the works of the law shall no man be justified" (Galatians 2:16); "A man is justified by faith without the deeds of the law" (Romans 3:28). The many Protestant sects are at various points of divergence from Roman Catholicism. At the furthest point of divergence stands Calvinism.

It is manifest that Protestantism is nothing else but what its name implies—a protest against the Roman Catholic

Church. The belief professed by both Protestants and Catholics that Jesus is the Messiah is really only a nominal basis for their rapprochement, for they have created many cults of personality around the central figure of Christianity. Reconciliation between the two main branches of Western Christianity would be possible only if both sides were willing to acquiesce in extensive revisions of basic doctrine involving the development of a new cult of personality for the alleged Messiah, Jesus.

Chapter 4

HISTORY AND HISTORICITY

In ordinary usage the word "history" has two connotations: (1) the actual events that occurred and (2) books describing and commenting on events their authors allege to have occurred.

Many a book contains statements pertaining to events the author believes occurred but whose chief subject does not concern past events. Such a book might deal with poetry, philosophy or science. But only those books mainly concerned with informing the reader about actual past events are called history; each is called a history, its author a historian.

Manifestly, actual events of the past were in no way ramifications of books in which they are described and explained. But most of our knowledge of past events—particularly those preceding our own lifetime—is acquired either through our reading of history or through communication, directly or "through the grapevine," with those who have read history.

The belief that history books contain nothing but hearsay evidence and that their authors fabricate events (or at any rate falsify and distort actual events to conform to their own preconceived notions) is probably what prompted Henry Ford to remark, "History is bunk." It is impossible that Henry Ford believed that the world's past, which constitutes history in one sense, is a figment of the imagination.

No doubt he meant that *recorded* history is "bunk" in that it is full of fallible opinion. But Henry Ford was renowned for his monumental ignorance of the history books he so scorned, having once publicly confounded Arnold Bennett, the author, with Benedict Arnold, the traitor.

Nevertheless, the fact that different accounts of an actual person's life are often at great variance with each other validates Henry Ford's remark as at least a partial truth. There can be no doubt that historians have imputed to actual persons of the past conceptual characteristics.

Present-day historians' disparate appraisals of King Richard III of England is a case in point. According to Shakespeare's *Richard III,* this king murdered his two nephews. Some historians agree with Shakespeare about this event; others disagree.

The Fellowship of the White Boar is an organization devoted to clearing Richard III's name of this and other charges, making a serious study of documents which throw light on Richard III and his contemporaries. The organization's avowed purpose is to expose Shakespeare's "base calumny." But if it is seeking evidence to exonerate Richard III, it is clear that it does not have what it is seeking. Hence the interesting psychological question is: why are the members of the Fellowship trying to clear Richard III's name? Apologies can no longer be made to either Richard III or his family. Nor is the character of Richard III still a partisan political issue in England as is, for example, that of the late President Roosevelt in the United States.

Since some historians say Richard III murdered his nephews and others deny this, it must be admitted that some of the events related in history are untrue. I use the word "historicity"—and I believe it is generally used in this sense —to mean the reality of all things, beings and events of the past. According to my word usage, any actual event, being or thing is *historic,* whether or not it has been described by historians. On the other hand, according to my word usage, all things, events and beings described in history are *historical,* whether or not they are historic. Therefore, even though some historians deny Richard III murdered his nephews, if they agree with my word usage they cannot deny this event is historical.

It is not difficult to understand why many historical things, beings and events are not historic. Historians acquire their information about the past mainly from the writings of other authors. The competent and honest historian must try to fix the period during which such an author lived; the intellectual climate in which his mind was conditioned; whether he was honest and competent; and whether he thought of himself as historian or writer of fiction. The historian should also try to determine whether a particular source of information was originally the work of only one author; if so, whether passages were deleted and others interpolated in editions published without the author's knowledge or consent. In short, historians are professional jurors of alleged events, things and beings of times gone by. With all the lying, half-truths and equivocation to which the ears of juries are subjected, it is likely that verdicts they render are often incorrect. It is the function of a jury to weigh the testimony presented by the witnesses, who, in contradistinction to the jury, are supposed to actually know something pertinent to the case at hand. But even honest witnesses often offer false testimony due to faulty recollection, poor vision or preconceived notions. How much more difficult than the weighing of testimony by a jury is the work of historians, who usually have not the testimony of witnesses to weigh, but can only consult the writings of other jurors of past events.

Unfortunately, each historian being human, he is not immune from being inculcated with hearsay opinion popular in his time and place. Addiction to hearsay opinion is a vice plaguing all mankind in every age and place. This failing is satirized in the remark of the Danish gravedigger in *Hamlet* that the madness of young Hamlet would not be noticed in England, where he has been sent, for there all the men are mad.

It should also be borne in mind that probably many historians are dishonest. Such persons are more than likely to falsify history, telling the public what they like to believe in order to curry their favor. For example, the American historian Julian Hawthorne, writing in the period immediately following the Spanish-American War, states in his *History of the United States*: "It is not too much to say that, since their history begins, there has been no female chastity in Spain, except by accident or under compulsion; nor any masculine honor, save that grotesque parody of honor which Spaniards are quick to assert, and which, with their 'pride,' renders them the solemn laughingstock of modern ages. Spanish rulers and the entire governing class, have always been types of inhumanity, tyranny and greed." Hawthorne, an educated man, must have known that his statement was untrue, despite the hatred existing against Spain in the United States at the time he was writing.

When historians discuss among themselves a person having a given name, how can they be sure they are talking about the same person? The name is not enough. Unless there is agreement concerning some unique event in the person's life or some special attribute of his, they can be certain they are talking about the same person only if they concur on a reproduction of his identities.

For example, as I have pointed out, Biblical scholars agree that at least two persons living two centuries apart wrote the material now combined in the Book of Isaiah. With regard to many verses in the book, however, uncertainty exists as to which of the two was the actual author. But if scholars discussing the authorship of such a verse agreed on a reproduction of the author's identities, they would know they are talking about the same person, even though they might be mistaken about this person being the author.

When the historicity of historical events in the life of an unidentifiable entity called by a unique name becomes questionable, it often happens that the very historicity of this entity becomes a subject for debate, as in the case of Shakespeare.

Many say Shakespeare was not historic. Some claim the author of "The Works of Christopher Marlowe" was also the author of "Shakespeare's Works" and that in his day he was called Christopher Marlowe. Others believe the author of "The Works of Francis Bacon" was also the author of "Shakespeare's Works" and that in his day he was called Francis Bacon. In the Parish Register in the Church of the Holy Trinity, Stratford-on-Avon, Warwickshire, however, it is recorded that in the year 1564 a person named William Shakespeare was born and baptized. The question is: were "Shakespeare's Works" written by the person named William Shakespeare who was born at Stratford-on-Avon in 1564 or by some other person? But even if it is true that either Bacon or Marlowe was the author of "Shakespeare's Works," it is probably erroneous to conclude that William Shakespeare was not historic. For there is no controversy about the unique fact that only one person christened with this name was baptized on a certain date in a particular place.

Even if historians have no difficulty in establishing a proper prerequisite for their discussion, this does not prove the historicity of the person under discussion. Indeed, he may be one of those historical persons who are conceptual, such as many believe King Arthur to be.

A written history of an actual person is called a biography. The biographer should either relate at least one event in his protagonist's life which he believes happened to only one historic person or discuss some unique characteristic of the person. Let us suppose he is writing a life of Shakespeare. If he believes *Henry IV* was written by more than one author, stating that Shakespeare wrote *Henry IV* will not suffice as a unique event in the protagonist's life. But if he states that William Shakespeare was born at Stratford-on-Avon in 1564 and was the only person christened with that name at that time in the Church of the Holy Trinity of that particular village, then he has established a premise for a biography and can go on to relate other events in the life of William Shakespeare, such as his composing part of *Henry IV*. If, however, the biographer believes *Henry IV* in its entirety was written by only one person, called William Shakespeare in his day, he will have established his premise by stating this to be a fact.

An historical novel is a fictional book in which, among other things, the life of an historical entity is discussed, but in which at least some of the events imputed to the life of this entity are admitted by the author to be imaginary. For example, no one would call Thomas Mann's *Joseph and His Brethren* a biography, but many would call it an historical novel. Mann takes a few pages of the Old Testament which recount the main events in the life of a person named Joseph and builds thereon a gigantic fictional edifice. Of course, many question the historicity of this Biblical character, claiming the original story about him is fictional. But even if we assume the Biblical story to be a true description of historic events, Mann's book is nonetheless largely fictional and is thus not a biography but a historical novel.

Regarding the biographies of the saints, a textbook used in Roman Catholic colleges makes this admission:

> Not a little of the same unintentional distortion, not to say caricature, appears in many of the lives of the saints, sometimes through pietistic misinterpretation, sometimes through uncritical blending of legend and fact. Not that legends are valueless. They have at least three great values: they weave the wizardry of poetry around

the great figures of the past; they are an appeal to the Catholic mind and will through the imagination; they are a key to the intelligence, temper and ideal of the people who used and invented them. Some of these legends are the result of the gumming on of pre-Christian hero stories to the lives of the saints; others are due to the mistakes of the biographers or of the people; others are due to a Christianized poetic imagination or to other causes.

The most extensive work in sifting fact from legend has been done by the Bollandist Fathers. Many other able scholars, both Catholic and non-Catholic, have in more recent decades accomplished very much in stripping away the legendary element that appears in the life of many of the saints and in presenting us with an account of them in their habits as they lived. Of practically all the modern saints we now have reliable and authentic lives, as we have of most of the prominent medieval saints and of some at least of even the saints and martyrs of the first three centuries.

How does the writer of this passage, who is convinced that in many biographies of the saints there is "uncritical blending of legend and fact," know that "we now have reliable and authentic lives of the saints"? Did not Catholics of the past who read biographies in which there is "uncritical blending of legend and fact" believe in the reliability of those biographies with a faith equal to his faith in the biographies of the saints written by the Bollandist Fathers? Furthermore, the Roman Catholics' claim that their faith is The One True Faith is not supported very well by the book's admission that legends (defined by the dictionary as fictitious or nonhistoric narrative) are useful in appealing to the Catholic imagination. If the historic lives of the saints were truly as admirable as is claimed, there should be no need to appeal to the imagination by "gumming on of pre-Christian hero stories to the lives of the saints." The truth about these lives should be exciting enough.

An interesting example of the naïveté of multitudes of Roman Catholics is afforded by the recent desanctification of Saint Philomena by the Sacred Congregation of Rites of the Roman Catholic Church.

The *Catholic Encyclopedia* says, "On the 25th of May, 1802, during a quest for graves of Roman martyrs in the catacomb of Priscilla, a tomb was discovered and opened; it contained a glass vessel and it was assumed to be a grave of a martyr. The view erroneously entertained in Rome that the presence of such vessels (supposed to have contained martyr's blood) in a grave was a symbol of martyrdom has been rejected in practice." Nevertheless, biographies have been written about this Philomena, imputing saintship to her. The authors of these biographies received their information from people who claimed to have had revelations about her; and many shrines have been dedicated to her.

On April 18, 1961, many Catholics were shocked by the following AP dispatch from Rome:

> The Sacred Congregation of Rites has ordered Philomena, the Martyred Virgin, stricken from the roll of Roman Catholic Saints.
>
> The Congregation said Philomena, venerated for a century and a half, had been neither a martyr nor a saint. The Congregation added that she had been venerated in error due to popular fervor rather than liturgical fact.
>
> Ecclesiastical authorities of the Diocese of Nola, near Naples, have been instructed to reconsecrate the church at nearby Mugnano del Cardinale, which has been the sanctuary and shrine of Philomena.

Children no longer may be baptized with the name Philomena—Filomena in Italian—which for years has been one of the most popular names for girls in southern Italy.

An article in the *New York Times,* April 21, 1961, reads in part as follows:

A Sacred Congregation of Rites in a recent "instruction" ordered the Feast of Philomena removed from liturgical calendars everywhere in the world. The names of St. Philomena churches would be changed in due course. Girls named Philomena will continue to be named Philomena, but will no longer have a Saint's Day to celebrate. They will be in the same position as everyone else baptized with a name not corresponding to a saint.

Past prayers to Philomena, if they were said with sincerity and faith, will retain their full effectiveness as though said to a true saint.

But long before the official desanctification of Philomena, Butler's *Lives of the Saints* admitted: "We do not know certainly whether she was in fact named Philomena in her earthly life, whether she was a martyr, whether her relics now rest in Mugnano or in some place unknown. And these questions are only of relative importance: the spiritual influence of her whom we call St. Philomena is what really matters." The author of this amazing statement in effect conceded that he did not know who or what the monad Philomena was when she was joined with a human entity; that he did not know whether the bones discovered were those of this entity; and that he did not even know her name. In short, he knew nothing about the life of the monad he was

83

writing about except that it was once joined with a woman's body. Yet he calls a monad about whose earthly life he knows nothing except that she was a woman "Philomena" and imputes "spiritual influence" to her.

When the writer of the article in Butler's *Lives of the Saints* wrote, "The spiritual influence of her whom we call St. Philomena is what really matters," did he know there was only one saintly monad in heaven who exerts spiritual influence over people and who had been a component of a woman-entity about whose life on earth nothing is known? If there are *two* such disembodied spirits in heaven, which is Philomena? If he were to call one such monad Philomena and the other one by another name, would he know which he is calling Philomena? His words "her whom we call Philomena" therefore can be meaningful only if the author believed that not more than one former woman-entity whose earthly life he knows nothing about exerts spiritual influence on people. And now that Philomena has been desanctified, even his assertion that she "exerts spiritual influence" is invalidated. Moreover, if the Sacred Congregation of Rites' knowledge of Philomena is not greater than that of the person who wrote about her in Butler's *Lives of the Saints,* then this organization does not know whom it has desanctified. There are people who know things about fictitious characters, but nobody seems to know anything about Philomena except that she was a woman. Therefore, today Philomena is not even a fictitious character.

But how do members of the Roman Catholic Church, whose leader is allegedly Christ's vicegerent on earth, become involved in a disputation on the sainthood of a monad whom they know nothing about? Indeed, why should there by any controversy in the Church about which monads are saints?

It should be understood that canonization of a saint is

simply a ceremony in which a monad is declared to be one of the saints in heaven; the monad was actually a saint before his canonization.

In order to determine whether a monad is a saint, the Sacred Congregation of Rites must depend on the judgment of fallible men such as archaeologists to unravel the true facts about his earthly life. How can they be certain this information is correct? The Sacred Congregation of Rites is thus merely a jury weighing the testimony of fallible witnesses who might be prejudiced. In Rome, investigations into the question of whether certain monads, such as Savonarola, are saints have been going on for years. Would it not be more efficacious for God, whom the Bible says spoke directly to many people, to speak directly to the Pope? He could easily inform him that certain monads are in fact among the saints in heaven, instead of allowing the Church to go to the expense and waste of time of long-drawn-out investigations. Could not this time and money be used for the collection and distribution of clothing and food to the poor?

And let it not be naïvely thought that the only reason for the canonization of saints is to pay them honor and inform the faithful regarding monads who are in a position to intercede for them with God. It is quite clear—even from the public statements of priests—that canonization often involves ulterior motives, national, racial or sexual in character. For example, on April 5, 1962 a consistory of cardinals meeting in the Vatican unanimously approved the canonization of Martin De Porres, a Negro who became a Dominican brother in the seventeenth century. Evidently, with the recent influx of African converts to the Church it is now considered propitious to placate the feelings of this downtrodden race by granting to it, through one of its members, a moral and spiritual excellence second to no other race. And behind the canonization of monads who were formerly women-entities, there is, no doubt, the motivation to present the Church as the champion of the weaker sex. Women outnumber men in both Church membership and attendance. In fact, they are the backbone of the Church. And the clergy well know it pays to inflate women's pride in their sex.

Chapter 5

THE HISTORICITY OF JESUS CHRIST

According to my word usage, Jesus is historical; the Gospel writers, who were undoubtedly historians, said he existed. But the historicity of Jesus is another matter.

The three words—Jehovah, Jesus and Allah—each thought by some to be God's exclusive name, are in reality nominal symbols correlated with three different recorded histories of God. Jews claim that wherever the name "Jehovah" appears in the Old Testament, reference is being made to God; Christians assert that wherever the word "Jesus" appears in the New Testament, reference is being made to God; and Mohammedans say that wherever the word "Allah" appears in their canonical books, reference is being made to God. Jews, Christians and Mohammedans disagree, not about the existence of God (for each of them teaches the existence of only one creator), but about the history of God, in which they concur only in part. For example, Jews and Mohammedans do not agree with Christians that God manifested Himself as a man; and Jews and Christians do not agree with Mohammedans that Mohammed was a prophet of God. But Jews and Christians at least formally agree that the Old Testament contains a completely accurate history of God.

According to the Trinitarian Christians, the human entity called Jesus in the New Testament was the earthly vessel of the Son of God-monad. But in Trinitarian Christian versions of the Bible the word "Jesus" is never used as a name for the Son of God-monad himself, only as the name of his human entity. Again, the word "Christ" is a Greek word meaning "anointed one," used by the New Testament as a title of Jesus; thus the words "Jesus" and "Christ" often appear there together as "Jesus Christ" or "Christ Jesus." But because of the confusion of the authors, the words "Jesus" and "Christ" also appear there separately, so that in some verses the word "Jesus" is the subject, while in others the word "Christ" is the subject. The word "Christ" has thus come to be thought of by some as another name of Jesus rather than a title associated with that name; and the words "Jesus," "Jesus Christ," "Christ Jesus," and "Christ" are thought of as having the same connotation, each referring to the human entity in which it is believed the Son of God-monad manifested himself to the perceptions of men.

Indeed, it is this entity, not the Son of God-monad per se, who is thought of as "our Lord." So far as I am aware, all biographies of "our Lord"—and it is said that more than three thousand such books exist—delineate not the history of the second person of the Triune Godhead either before he manifested himself as a human entity on earth or after the entity's ascent to heaven, but only that period of his history in which he was manifested as a human entity on earth.

Again, the Trinitarian Christians say that the entity Jesus Christ was the earthly vessel of God. But all debates about the historicity of Jesus Christ quite properly concern themselves not with his divinity but with the question of the historicity of the words and deeds imputed by the New Testament to the human entity it calls Jesus Christ.

Christianity differs from other religions in that the latter only require their adherents to practice certain rituals and behave in accordance with certain moral principles; they do not require them to believe any part of the history of God.

Regarding this, Schopenhauer, in his *Essay on the Christian System*, says:

> Christianity has this peculiar disadvantage, that, un-
> like other religions, it is not a pure system of doctrine:
> its chief and essential feature is that it is a history, a
> series of events, a collection of facts, a statement of the
> actions and sufferings of individuals: it is this history
> which constitutes dogma, and belief in it is salvation.
> Other religions, Buddhism, for instance, have, it is true,
> historical appendages, the life, namely of their founders:
> this, however, is not part and parcel of the dogma, but
> is taken along with it.

Philo was one of many distinguished first-century historians who did not mention Jesus in their writings. What then were the sources of information, other than the New Testament, which the three thousand biographers of Jesus consulted?

The Roman historian Tacitus mentions Jesus Christ not because he knew anything about him, but because he knew about the Christians and their professed belief in Christ. A passage in his *Annals,* composed about 116 C.E., reads:

> A persistent rumor associated Nero with the starting
> of this fire [the great fire in Rome in 64 C.E.]. To com-
> bat this he decided to provide culprits and inflicted the
> most atrocious tortures upon the sect known as Chris-
> tians, detested by the people for their practices. Their
> name is derived from one Christ, who was condemned
> to be crucified by the procurator Pontius Pilate in the
> reign of Tiberius. This pernicious sect, formerly pro-
> scribed, has established itself not only throughout Judea,
> where it originated, but in the very City [Rome] itself.

In the extant editions of the voluminous *Jewish Antiqui-*

ties of Josephus Flavius (born in 37 C.E.) are fifteen and a half lines about Jesus:

> Now there was about this time Jesus, a
> wise man; if it be lawful to call him a man;
> for he was a doer of wonderful works, and a
> teacher of such men as receive the truth
> with pleasure. He drew over to him both many
> of the Jews and many of the Gentiles. He
> was the Christ. And when Pilate, at the
> suggestion of the principal men among us,
> had condemned him to the cross, those that
> loved him at the first did not forsake him:
> for he appeared to them alive again, the
> third day: as the divine prophets had
> foretold these and ten thousand wonderful
> things concerning him. And the tribe
> of Christians, so named from him, is not
> extinct at this day.

But not one of the Church fathers prior to Eusebius, such as Chrysostom and Origen, who read and quoted Josephus, says anything about this passage. Indeed, Origen wrote that there is nothing regarding Jesus in the writings of Josephus. Eusebius (born 264 C.E.) was the first of the Church Fathers to quote this passage from the writings of Josephus. However, one of the chapters of Eusebius' *Proe paratio Evangelica* is titled "How far it may be proper to use falsehood as a medium for the benefit of those who require to be deceived." Elsewhere he says, "I have repeated whatever may redound to the glory, and suppressed all that could tend to the disgrace of our religion." Therefore, the consensus of scholars is that the passage about Jesus in Josephus is an interpolation, and that Eusebius, whose own writings attest to his dishonesty, was probably the culprit. Even present-day Christian

90

theologians concede the original writings of Josephus contained nothing about Jesus. But time was when this pitiful passage was used by theologians to refute the infidel's taunt that the Man of Nazareth was mythical.

But for the moment let us assume Josephus did write these lines. The first question that comes to mind is: if Jesus was a "doer of wonderful works" and if "He was the Christ" why did Josephus, born in Palestine only a few years after Jesus' alleged death and resurrection, write only fifteen and a half lines about him? When Josephus was a mature man, there should have been many people in Palestine who remembered Jesus and his "wonderful works," and from whom this historian could have received much more detailed information than he seems to have had. One would think that if Josephus really believed "Jesus . . . was the Christ" he would have devoted at least half of his book to a description of his life! Furthermore, the statement "Those that loved him at the first did not forsake him" contradicts the New Testament narrative which relates that the disciples Judas Iscariot and Peter *did* forsake him.

It therefore appears that the biographers of Jesus could have obtained no authentic information about his life from the writings of any historians save the Gospel writers. And if the Gospels contain the only reliable account of the life of Jesus that has come down to us from ancient times, why should any other biographies of him have been written? Indeed, these other biographies are in reality historical novels, containing as they do accounts of events in the life of Jesus which are nothing but the imaginings of their authors.

Many claim the Gospel writers created a conceptual entity they called Jesus Christ. Is there any meaning in this assertion?

In order to answer this question, first let us analyze the confusion often caused by the use of proper names to desig-

nate real and conceptual entities. Suppose Mr. A. were to say
to Mr. B. that Santa Claus is a real human being. Mr. B.
might laugh at this assertion. But how does he know it is
not true? If Mr. B. scornfully retorts that no human being
has ever flown through the air on a sleigh drawn by a team
of reindeers, Mr. A. might agree, but point out that lies have
been told about many persons, among them perhaps Mr. B.
himself. Does Mr. B. think he is nonexistent just because
people impute to his life things which are purely imaginary?
Perhaps Mr. B. is a member of the Fellowship of the White
Boar. Was Richard III nonexistent simply because lies have
been told about him?

The reason Messrs. A. and B. disagree is that the words
"Santa Claus" do not mean the same thing to them; so they
are not arguing about the same thing. It is meaningless for
them to argue about the existence of one and only one entity
—Santa Claus—unless Mr. A. makes assertions about certain
unique characteristics or events in the life of an entity he
calls Santa Claus, and Mr. B. asserts that nobody with any
of the unique characteristics of the entity Mr. A. calls
Santa Claus is historic. If Mr. B. cannot refute all of Mr. A.'s
assertions, he will not have proved the nonexistence of the
entity Mr. A calls Santa Claus. However, if Mr. A. says Santa
Claus did something unique at a certain place at a certain time,
Mr. B., in order to refute this assertion, need only prove that
nobody has done this thing at either the time or the place
Mr. A claims Santa Claus did it; Mr. B. need not necessarily
prove that nobody has ever done this thing in any place at any
time.

On the other hand, suppose Mr. A. makes only the following assertion about the uniqueness of Santa Claus: that he
is an old man with a long white beard who goes about at
Christmastime giving toys to small children. If Mr. B. can
show there is more than one man doing this, he will have
disproved the uniqueness of the entity Mr. A. calls Santa

Claus, thereby vitiating the basis for their argument.

To repeat, if Mr. A. makes assertions about a unique characteristic of an entity he calls Santa Claus, and Mr. B. is not certain whether or not a person with such a characteristic exists, Mr. B. cannot disprove the existence of this person merely by showing it is a physical impossibility for reindeers to draw a sleigh through the air.

As to Jesus, it is meaningless for two people to debate his onetime existence on earth unless the believer makes specific assertions about unique characteristics of Jesus or unique events in his life and if all these assertions are denied by the nonbeliever. If the believer says that everything in the New Testament is historic, then for the nonbeliever to prove the nonexistence of Jesus it is necessary to show that no Jew living in Palestine during the reign of Augustus Caesar had any of the unique characteristics or history attributed to him by the New Testament. If, for example, the nonbeliever concedes it is conceivable that during that period one and only one Jew drove money-changers out of the temple in Jerusalem, then he cannot rightly assert that Jesus is not historic.

Nevertheless, recent scholarship has brought to light much evidence that unique events in the lives of two real entities who did not live at the same time have been conflated in the New Testament, as though they happened to only one entity —the names of these two entities having been subsumed under the name "Jesus." A. Powell Davies, in *The First Christian,* points out that Acts 5:30 says that Jesus was hanged on a tree, which conflicts with the Gospel story of the crucifixion. Davies correlates Acts 5:30 with the *Talmud* and the *Toldoth Yeschu,* which mention a certain Yeschu who was born during the reign of the Priest-King Alexander Jannaeus (104-76 B.C.E.) and was hanged on a tree. Says Davies:

There is a betrayal in the toldoth, as there is in the

New Testament; also a crown of thorns, vinegar to drink and a number of other parallels with the gospels; but Jesus is quite definitely hanged, not crucified, and is buried on a Sunday, not a Friday. . . . Putting the story together (to the extent this is possible) from the Jewish writings, what we have is a Jesus who fled to Egypt during the reign of Alexander Jannaeus (who crucified eight hundred Pharisees, and we do not know what he may have done to the Essenes), returning to Judea after the king's death, and perishing during the reign of Queen Salome (Alexandra) at the hands of the wicked high priest.

This story parallels the New Testament story of the flight into Egypt caused by King Herod's desire to destroy the new-born Messiah. Indeed, the conflation of the histories of the two entities is also evident from conflicting statements of Epiphanius, fourth-century Bishop of Salamis, that Christ was born during the reign of Alexander Jannaeus and also of Herod the Great.

Thanks to recent discoveries and patient study by scholars, therefore, it seems overwhelmingly evident that the original composition of part of the New Testament predates the era following the death of the so-called canonical Jesus (born during the reign of Herod the Great), in which all of the New Testament was heretofore believed to have been originally composed; and that much that is imputed to the life of the canonical Jesus in the New Testament is actually taken from these earlier writings concerning an entity who lived approximately a century before him.

Chapter 6

NAMES OF MONADS AND ENTITIES

A name is a sound associated with a monad, in order to expedite communication of information pertaining to it, without denoting it. A monad's name is extrinsic to it. It is a covenience, like a walking stick, which is a possession, not a part, of the person who carries it. A name which designates a monad is usually retained regardless of what offices or positions this monad may occupy at different periods of its life.

Titles, such as father, doctor or general, are not names of particular monads, but rather designations of offices or positions. Thus, Eisenhower was at one time a colonel, afterward a general, later a university president and finally a president of his country. Yet throughout his life he has retained one name. But entities other than Eisenhower have occupied the offices he has occupied and have had associated with their names the same titles which have been associated with his name.

When one addresses a monad who bears a title he often addresses him by that title. Thus, people talking directly to Eisenhower might address him as "General." But no one would call Eisenhower "General" when speaking about him to a third person. When one speaks in the third person it is ambiguous for him to use a title without an associated name, unless either he or his listener is oriented to only one monad with that title. Thus, one might speak of his mother as

"Mother." Similarly, a person might speak of the present President of the United States as "the President." When speaking of a previous President of the United States, however, he would have to specify that president by name, otherwise one would not know which president he is referring to.

The words Buddha and Christ are titles, not names. Many men were called Buddha. The most famous was Gautama. Yet people often speak of "Buddha" as having said this or done that. If they are referring to Gautama, they ought to use his name. Likewise, why should people say "Christ" did this or "Christ" said that? This usage is apt to mislead people into thinking "Christ" is Jesus' family name.

It may be objected that it is universally understood that "Christ" refers to the last and greatest of those who bore that title: that God Himself was manifested in a man and as such is eternally the Christ, this entity having supplanted all previous Christs. But the whole *raison d'être of* titles and offices is classification. If only one entity exists who has supplanted all previous ones in bearing a title, and he continues to carry this title throughout eternity, it is plain his title has become meaningless: for the class of entities it designates is defunct. Therefore, the title Christ (Messiah) is meaningful only as the designation of an office which *was* extant, not as the designation of an office extant *today*. Furthermore, the Supreme Being, either as a pure spirit or anthropomorphic phenomenon, cannot possibly have any congener. It is thus illogical to associate a title with the name of the entity in which He was a component.

It is significant, moreover, that Jesus called himself "a prophet," not "the prophet": "But Jesus said unto them, A prophet [speaking of himself as well as of others] is not without honour, but in his own country, and among his own kin, and in his own house." (Mark 6:4). His words "a prophet" indicate that he thought of his mission not as something unique, but as a sort of social service which had been

96

performed by many congeners in the class of entities called "prophets." It is thus incorrect to say that Jesus thought of himself as a God-monad.

Again, the proper purpose of names, as distinct from titles, is to designate by unique sounds monads or entities as such, not the rank or office to which these monads or entities have attained. But names have never been exclusively thought of as expedients of social intercourse. In the *Golden Bough,* Frazer comments on primitive man's attitude toward names:

> Unable to discriminate clearly between words and things, the savage commonly fancies that the link between a name and the person or thing denominated by it is not a mere arbitrary and ideal association, but a real and substantial bond which unites the two in such a way that magic may be wrought on a man just as easily through his name as through his hair, his nails, or any other material part of his person. In fact, primitive man regards his name as a vital portion of himself and takes care of it accordingly. Thus, for example, the North American Indian regards his name, not as a mere label, but as a distinct part of his personality, just as much as are his eyes or his teeth, and believes that injury will result as surely from the malicious handling of his name as from a wound inflicted on any part of his organism.

In the New Testament are many passages revealing a jealous, possessive attitude toward names not much different from that imputed by Frazer to "the savage." For example, this remarkable verse in the Book of Revelation: "He that hath an ear, let him hear what the Spirit saith unto the churches; To him that overcometh will I give to eat of the hidden manna, and will give him a white stone, and in the stone a new name written, which no man knoweth saving he that receiveth it" (Rev. 2:17). Evidently, the writer of this verse thought that the salvation of a believer whose body has passed on to the grave is contained in a new name which becomes part and parcel of his spirit-organism through his exclusive knowledge of this name. Certainly a name known to only one monad is of no value as an expedient of social intercourse.

As I have said, perhaps many Jews believe it is possible to project a deceased person's essence into a new-born infant by giving him the same name.

Jesus himself seems to have shared with other men their superstitious belief in the magic which can be wrought through names: "For where two or three are gathered together in my name there am I in the midst of them" (Matthew 18:20). Which of his names was he talking about? His Hebrew name, "Joshua"? Its Greek equivalent, "Jesus"? Or "Immanuel," the name by which the Christians believe the Old Testament designates him?

In Biblical times people were generally given derivative names, that is, names derived from other words.[1] Thus, the Biblical name "Isaac" is derived from the Hebrew word for laughter, for Isaac's mother, Sarah, laughed when she was told that she would have a child at the age of ninety. The name "Israel," which means "he strove with God," is an agnomination of the patriarch Jacob, who wrestled with an angel representing God. The name "Esau," derived from the Hebrew word for hair, is attributive, for Esau was a hairy person. It is thus clear that ancient man was accustomed to assigning persons derivative names which were either attributive or expressive of some unique event in their lives. Sometimes, however, an individual had more than one name, as in the case of Jacob.

[1] The difference between derivative and nonderivative words is illustrated, for example, by the trade name "No-Cal," obviously derived from "no calories," and the trade name "Kodak," which, as far as is known, is a unique name bearing no semblance to any word in any language. Kodak is purely a designatory word, having no derivation.

The age-old habit of personifying thoughts by mentally projecting them through names into people and other creatures who by demeanor or looks reflect these thoughts is illustrated by Poe's celebrated poem, "The Raven," said to have been inspired by the death of a sweetheart. Poe names a sculptured bird hanging over his door "Nevermore." The poet's terrified mental state caused by his realization of the finality of his separation from his sweetheart, plus the indifference of the universe to his anguish, are expressed in the bird's automatic croaking of the word "nevermore" and in its open, unseeing eyes, having "the seeming of a demon that is dreaming."

In modern times many people bear the same derivative names. But rarely does a person's name express any of his attributes or a portion of history peculiarly associated with him, except insofar as it may be the name of a relative. Many persons of different races, nationalities, temperaments and family histories bear the same name. Nowadays, many men are named Isaac; but their name is not thought of as expressing a laughable event in their lives.

Eventually it was realized that instead of calling a person "William the son of Robert," it was more practical for William to have two names—a given name and a family cognomen. In this system fewer names are necessary; for even if many persons bear the same first name, and many bear the same family cognomen, a combination of a particular first name and a particular family cognomen is usually unique. At any rate, one does not usually know two or more persons having the same combination of first name and family cognomen. When this does occur, they are usually assigned nicknames or aliases. Such an unusual situation exists in Quebec, Canada, where fifteen thousand people out of a population of sixty thousand bear the family cognomen "Tremblay." The apparent explanation is that many members of one family settled in Quebec and multiplied.

Aliases are often used by persons who wish to hide their past from the members of a community to which they have fled.

Pseudonyms are sometimes used by famous persons who wish to avoid intrusion by the public into their lives. But when an author, portrait painter or composer chooses to use a pseudonym, it is his duty to posterity to use the same pseudonym consistently, thereby lessening the possibility of confusion about his work.

Therefore, it is obvious that knowing a name and the reported deeds or attributes of the entity bearing that name does not necessarily entail knowing the entity. In short, a name is not an identity.

But even though civilized man no longer thinks of his name as a vital part of his organism, a person's name is often considered significant because of the association of ideas it conveys. For example, an AP dispatch from Rome, December 6, 1959, stated:

> Pope John XXIII said he was pleased to see Maj. John S. D. Eisenhower at President Eisenhower's Vatican audience today "because of the happy and encouraging coincidence" that his name was the same as the Pope's. "The name John, which in its Biblical significance means 'gift of God,' expresses, in fact, confidence, joy, and serene robustness," the Pontiff remarked.

And who does not remember the fanfare stirred up at the time of the coronation of the present Queen of England by the circumstance that her name was Elizabeth? This event was hailed as signaling the advent of a new "Elizabethan" era, expected to equal in greatness the previous era of the same name. The name which evokes in the hearts of Englishmen nostalgic thoughts about their country's past achievements at the time of the 1953 coronation strengthened their faith in the renascence of national glory. Thus by the chance (or providential) accession to a throne of a person with a name having historical significance is the unity of a people reinforced.

In *The Importance of Being Ernest,* Oscar Wilde satirizes humanity's excessive preoccupation with such trivia as names. In this play, a young lady decides that the man she marries must be named Ernest, for this name inspires her with confidence.

Some people even go so far as to change their names to conform with the euphony of the language indigenous to the country to which their parents migrated. These people evidently think that by beautifying their names, often with the change of but one letter, they thereby also beautify themselves, or at least render themselves more acceptable to their neighbors. In our own country, where Anglophiles are preponderant, are innumerable people having continental-sounding names who think—perhaps with good reason—that their names are inimical to their general social advancement. Some of them change the pronunciation of their names without changing the spelling. As is well known, a prominent public figure bearing the German name "Strauss" (the "au" of which is ordinarily pronounced as in "kraut") has anglicized its pronunciation to "straws," without changing its spelling.

A beautiful name is still thought of as an asset even for a girl naturally endowed with beauty. It is likely that many derivative names were originated by lovers who, on seeing their paramours, were reminded of certain pleasant thoughts. To one whose ear has been conditioned from earliest childhood in the English language, the following names are the quintessence of euphony and beauty: Rosalind; Claire; Joyce; Grace; Mona; Estelle; June; Gale. Rosalind reminds one of roses in a glen; Joyce of joy; Mona of the moon; June of a

101

summer day, peace and tranquillity; Claire of light and clarity; Estelle of starlight; Grace of freedom and the blessings of God; Gale of the naked beauty and strength of a storm, the primal catharsis of nature. The pseudonym "Tempest Storm," the stage name of a certain lady of the burlesque theater, has much the same impact of "Gale."

Stratford, we have said, is the name of the village in England in which Shakespeare was born. In recent years, theaters devoted exclusively to the presentation of Shakespeare's works have been built in Stratford, Connecticut, and Stratford, Ontario. Such theaters could just as well have been built in large cities. But the organizers of these projects understood psychology. It seems that the name Stratford has such drawing power that the inconvenience of traveling to these small towns is ignored by the Shakespeare fans, who flock to the summer festivals in droves. The Bard's own question:

> What's in a name? that which we call a rose
> By any other name would smell as sweet

has thus been answered by his public.

Chapter 7

THE NAME OF GOD

Some of the names the ancient Israelites assigned to God are functional or attributive. For example: dayyan (judge); shadday (almighty) ; zaddik (righteous) ; hannun (gracious); rahum (merciful); and Elohim (chief). Maimonides, foremost apologist for Judaism during the Middle Ages, points out that most names of God are derivative. For example, "Adonay," the name most commonly used by the Jews for God, was derived from the Hebrew appellative for "master."

Maimonides asserts that the Hebrew name described as the "tetragrammaton"[1] is the only nonderivative name of God in the Old Testament, although many attempts have been made to attach meaning to it. He further states that it is the name only of the divine monad.

As I have stated, the Israelites first thought of the name "Jehovah" as being that of their patron god, but eventually came to think of it as the name of God. When reading the Bible aloud, the Jews substituted "Adonay" for "Jehovah," since "Jehovah" was considered too holy to be uttered by anyone except the priests in the sanctuary of the temple on the

[1]The English word "tetragrammaton" is a metonym for the *nomen propium* transliterated "Jehovah." In Hebrew this name consists of four consonants. (The Greek word for "four" is *"tetra."*)

In Hebrew, vowels consist of configurations of dots and dashes under the consonants. These vowels often are omitted for the convenience of printing, since most people who read Hebrew recognize words by their consonants.

holy days. The verses "Thou shalt not take the name of the Lord thy God in vain" (Exodus 20:7) and "He that blasphemeth the name of the Lord, he shall surely be put to death" (Leviticus 24:16) were interpreted as forbidding for all time the uttering of "Jehovah" by any person other than a priest. Indeed, to this day the Jews do not utter the holy name. Nevertheless, they are permitted to utter its abbreviated form, "Jah." The word "hallelujah" consists of "hallelu" ("give praise to") and "Jah": thus, "hallelujah" means "give praise to Jehovah."

Maimonides, quoting Rabbi Eliezer, made the absurd assertion that the name "Jehovah" always existed, that in the beginning was "the name of God" and "God." When only God existed, only He could have known His name. Why, then, did he need a name? Names being expedients by which each monad distinguishes "I" from the various "thous," they could have had no utility until at least two monads existed besides God. Before the creation, God had no reason even to think of Himself as "I," for none existed whom He could have addressed as "thou."

There is no disagreement about the descriptive metonym "tetragrammaton." There is, however, controversy about the vowels under the four consonants. Some transliterate the tetragrammaton as "Yahweh." Many Trinitarian Christians, alarmed by the recent expansion of "Jehovah's Witnesses," have resorted to the argument that Yahweh—not Jehovah—is the correct transliteration of the tetragrammaton; therefore, they argue, Jehovah's Witnesses are not the true church of God.

The notion that there are correct and incorrect transliterations into English of words from other alphabetical systems is based on a misunderstanding. It is not always possible to transliterate a word from one alphabetical system to another with phonetic accuracy. As to transliterations of words into English (which unlike German, is a nomic, homonymous language), the notion that the spelling of these words is infallible is particularly erroneous, since in English there are no universal rules relating phonetics and spelling.

In my discussion, I use the transliteration "Jehovah" consistently.

The Jehovah-Yahweh controversy is certainly more foolish than the Jesus-Joshua controversy. Some claim that the Hebrew name of Jesus was the same as that of the protagonist whose life is described in the Old Testament Book of Joshua, and whose name is transliterated "Joshua" in all English versions of the Bible. There is validity to the question, "Why are the names of two entities whose Hebrew names are spelled the same way not transliterated with the same spelling within each English version of the Christian Bible?" The transliteration within the covers of one book of this Hebrew name as "Joshua" wherever one entity is mentioned and as "Jesus" wherever the other is mentioned creates the false impression that the two entities had different Hebrew names. It is likely that the Christian translators created the verbal distinction so that in theological discussions the two entities would not be confounded.

Regarding the name "Jehovah," Webster's Twentieth Century Dictionary states: "Jehovah, *n.* Lord; the specific name of God considered as the special deity of the Hebrews; usually rendered the Lord in English translations of the Old Testament. The name is of unknown meaning."

An example of the nonsense which results from the substitution of "the Lord" for "Jehovah" is afforded by Psalms 16:2, where the Hebrew words transliterated as "Adonay" and "Jehovah" are both rendered "Lord," so that the verse reads: "I have said unto the Lord: 'Thou art my Lord.' " Would it not be inane for a child to say, "O Mother, Thou art my mother"?

And since each of the three major monotheistic religions uses one of the three names—Jehovah, Allah or Jesus—to the

105

exclusion of the others to designate the one and only Supreme Being, the creator of all men, is it not illogical to consider Jehovah as "the special deity of the Hebrews," as the dictionary puts it? Nevertheless, the dictionary's statement is perfectly consonant with the fallacious thinking so widespread on the subject of God and His name.

This thinking is basically a ramification of the desire of each religious group to think of Him as the sponsor of their own religion and none other. Each group's belief in an exclusive bond between it and God is thus expressed by the imaginary conjunction of His essence with one and only one name. Thus, the Christians think of the name "Jesus" as being the name of "our Lord" and the Jews think of the name "Jehovah" as the name of "our God." The Jews have good reason to say that the name "Jesus" is not the name of "our God," since they do not believe that the entity whom the writers of the New Testament call Jesus was a human manifestation of God. But the Christians have no valid reason to say that the name "Jehovah" is not the name of "our God," since they believe the monad for whose name they substitute the appellative "the Lord" in their English renditions of the Old Testament is one of the "persons" of the Triune Godhead—the Father.

The average Trinitarian Christian erroneously believes that often when the word "Lord" appears in the Old Testament, Jesus is being referred to. For example, the verse in Psalms 110 which in Trinitarian versions reads:

> The Lord saith unto my Lord:
> "Sit thou at My right hand,
> Until I make thine enemies thy footstool"

is used as proof that the existence of two persons of the Triune Godhead is implicit in the Old Testament. What they fail to realize is that in Hebrew the first word of this verse

106

translated "Lord" is "Jehovah," the other being the possessive of the general appellative for "lord". The true translation of "The Lord saith unto my Lord" is, therefore,
"Jehovah saith unto my lord," "lord" being in no sense a
reference to God. The Trinitarian Christians are thus mistaken in believing that this verse is prophetic—that Jesus'
ascension to heaven to sit at the right hand of the Father
was its fulfillment.

Chapter 8

INVOKING THE NAME OF GOD

All primitive peoples believe that merely by invoking the
name of their god they automatically command his services.
Regarding this, Frazer says:

> Hence just as the furtive savage conceals his real name
> because he fears that sorcerers might make an evil use
> of it, so he fancies that his gods must likewise keep their
> true name secret, lest other gods or even men should
> learn the mystic sounds and thus be able to conjure with
> them. . . . Nowhere was the crude conception of the
> secrecy and magical virtue of the divine name more
> firmly held or more fully developed than in ancient
> Egypt. . . . Isis wormed his secret name from Ra, the
> great Egyptian god of the Sun. . . . And she meditated
> in her heart saying, "Cannot I by virtue of the great
> name Ra make myself a goddess and reign like him in
> heaven and earth?" For Ra had many names, but the
> great name that gave him all power over gods and men
> was known to none but himself.

The Bible itself contains evidence that primitive men
thought they could force gods to serve them by invoking their
true names; for this reason gods were reluctant to divulge
their names even to their most trusted servants: "And I ap-

108

peared unto Abraham, unto Isaac and unto Jacob; by the name of Shadday; but my name Jehovah was not made known to them" (Exodus 6:3) . According to the Bible, Jehovah at first withheld his true name even from Moses when he spoke to him out of the burning bush. Martin Buber, one of Judaism's foremost contemporary apologists, says, "Moses expected the people in their distress to ask him what was the name of the god as whose messenger he spoke (not what was the name of the 'God of their fathers'!) (Exodus 3:13). For according to the usage common to primitive peoples, once they seized the secret of the name they could conjure the god, and coerce him to manifest himself to them and serve them." Exodus 3:14 says that when Moses asked Jehovah what his name was, he received the reply, "I am that I am" or more accurately "I will be that I will be." Only when Moses ascended to the top of Mount Sinai to receive the two tables of the Law did Jehovah reveal his name to him: "And the Lord descended in the cloud, and stood with him there, and proclaimed the name of the Lord" (Exodus 34:5). And the Israelites imputed great power to this name: " 'So shall they put My name upon the children of Israel, and I will bless them' " (Numbers 6:27).

The New Testament, quoting the Old Testament Book of Joel (3:5), says, "Whosoever shall call on the name of the Lord shall be saved" (Acts 2:21; Romans 10:13). But the proper translation of Joel 3:5 is: "And it shall come to pass that whosoever shall call on the name Jehovah shall be saved." It is evident that the author of the Book of Acts was unaware of this, for in verses 4:10-12 he says, "Be it known unto you all, and to all the people of Israel, that by the name Jesus Christ . . . even by him doth this man stand here before you whole . . . for there is none other name under heaven given among men, whereby we must be saved." Which, then, is the "Open sesame" through which one is saved—Jesus or Jehovah? Which name is referred to in Hebrews 6:10? ("For God is not unrighteous to forget your work and labor of love, which ye showed toward his name.") And does the "Open sesame" consist of uttering the proper phonetic sounds of the name?

To this day it is believed that great power can be evoked by uttering the name "Jesus." A quotation from a Roman Catholic brochure reads: "A plenary Apostolic Indulgence can be gained at the hour of death by those who commend their souls devoutly to God and accept death with resignation, having confessed and received Holy Communion, or if that be impossible, invoke the most Holy Name of Jesus in their hearts if they cannot do it with their lips." And an article in the *New York Times* of January 4, 1960 reads, in part:

> Invoking the name of Jesus was urged yesterday by the Rev. Oscar V. Lynch as a means of overcoming temptations. He preached at the 10 A.M. solemn mass in St. Patrick's Cathedral. . . . During times of temptations, sickness and disappointments he commended repeating the name of Jesus for sustenance. . . . "If we would but utter the Holy Name of Jesus, the sound of it would send the tempter screaming back to Hell." . . . Father Lynch said that from the earliest day of the Roman Catholic Church the name of Jesus Christ had always been devoutly displayed. Many indulgences, he said, can be gained by devout invocation of the name.

The great Biblical verse "And the Lord will be king over all the earth: on that day shall the Lord be one and his name one" (Zechariah 14:9) shows its author's deep insight into the tragic conflict which often results from the use and misuse of words. The prophet probably meant that in the end of days all peoples will not only be monotheists but will understand that God being called by many names causes

110

much misunderstanding. But the prophet failed to hurdle the last obstacle to the ultimate resolution of the problem of the name of God—that the designating of the Supreme Being by a proper name is a habit rooted in the past, when conceptual monads such as national and patron gods were named in order to differentiate between them.[1]

---

[1] This ancient way of thinking is illustrated by a verse of the prophet Micah, who lived long before Zechariah:

"For let all the peoples walk each one
in the name of its god,
But we will walk in the name of the
Lord our God forever and ever" (4:5).

Notice that in English versions of this verse the lower case letter "g" is used in the word for the patron monad of each of the peoples ("god"); the capital letter "G" is used for the Jews' ("our") patron monad. The implication of the translator is that the patron monad of the Jews is the creator of the universe, in contradistinction to the patron monads of "the peoples." This implication is certainly not derived from the original Hebrew, in which there are no upper or lower case letters, all characters being of identical size.

Chapter 9

RECEIVING CHRIST

It is one thing to know a monad's name or title, another thing to know the monad himself or his essence.

In his *Essay Concerning Human Understanding,* John Locke writes,

> For, men being furnished with words, by the common language of their countries, can scarce be ignorant of those which their neighbors have occasion frequently to mention to them, out of an opinion either of the dignity of the subject, or the concernment everyone is thought to have of being acquainted with it, and therefore, it is altogether impossible that the name of God being once mentioned in any part of the world to express some superior invisible being, but that, from the reason men will always have to mention it often, it should spread far and wide; and be continued down to all generations, and never be lost again, though the general reception of his name, and some imperfect and unsteady notions conveyed thereby, proves nothing more but that he who first framed in his mind this notion named it and taught it others, had thought maturely of the causes of things, and traced them to this original; and had withal broached to the world a notion and

taught a name, which mankind would be ever after concerned to retain and propagate.

But it being most evident that men of the same country under one and the same name of God have far different nay often contrary ideas and conceptions of him, their agreeing in a name or sound will scarce prove any innate notion of him. . . . And this universality of consent, so much urged, if it proved any native impressions, it will be only this: that God imprinted on thousands of men speaking the same language, a name for himself, but not any idea; since those nations agreed only in the name, but had far different apprehensions about the thing itself.

What Locke is saying, in part, is that people have different notions about an unknown superior monad—"some superior invisible being"—even though they may all call him by the same name. But if people have different notions about this unknown superior monad, how could Locke have been certain they all refer to the same being? Angels, for example, are also thought of as superior invisible beings. Unless they agree on some unique attribute or event in the life of this monad, there is no reason to believe they are talking about the same monad. If, then, they agree that "God" has created all things—a unique act which can be imputed to only one monad—they are definitely talking about the same being no matter how differently they may think of Him in other respects.

Even when one thinks about a monad who is a component of a visible being, does this necessarily indicate he knows this entity? One can believe in the existence of an entity having a particular history or attribute without knowing any of its identities. And vice versa, one can know an entity without knowing anything about it other than its identities. It also often happens that one knows something about an

113

entity, and also knows the entity, without realizing this entity is the one about whom he knows this particular fact.

God is certainly not known by those who have never perceived Him physically, although they may know about Him. The New Testament relates that when the Apostle Paul was in Athens he saw an altar with an inscription reading: "TO THE UNKNOWN GOD" (Acts 17:23). Evidently, in addition to the gods known to them through statues, certain Athenians believed in the existence of a super monad unknown to anyone through identities. Paul must have thought he and the Athenians worshiped the same monad, for he said, "Whom therefore ye ignorantly worship him declare I unto you." But what could Paul have meant by saying the Athenians were ignorant of the one they worshiped? If he meant they did not *know* "him," this could rightly be said of anyone who never perceived God physically. On the other hand, if he meant they did not know *about* "him," how could he be sure they worshiped the same monad as he? How did he know they were not worshiping an angel, using the word "god" to designate this monad? Did Paul know the word "god" had the same meaning in the minds of the Athenians that it had in his mind? If, however, the Athenians thought of the Greek word rendered "God" in this verse as meaning the creator of all things, they *did* know about Him.

In the sixth century B.C.E., thousands of Jews fleeing from Palestine before the Babylonian hordes took refuge in Egypt. Many became corrupted by the Egyptian custom of offering incense to "the queen of heaven" (Jeremiah 44). The prophet Jeremiah, among the refugees in Egypt, vilified the delinquent Jews who adopted this practice and prophesied the Lord would annihilate them if they did not mend their ways.

Now, for the greater part of the Christian era the Catholics have been praying to "the queen of heaven." They believe there has been only one queen of heaven, who on earth was

114

a component of an entity called Mary who gave birth to Jesus..

For the moment let us assume that Roman Catholicism is the true faith. Mary, the mother of Jesus, did not come into existence (was not "conceived," as the Catholics put it) before the first century B.C.E. Therefore, no queen of heaven existed in the sixth century B.C.E. and Jews of that period who prayed to "the queen of heaven" were praying to a conceptual, nonexistent monad.

Let us suppose that the delinquent Jews who prayed to "the queen of heaven" instructed their children to do likewise, and in this manner the same thoughts and practices relating to "the queen of heaven" were perpetuated generation after generation among non-Christian Jews well into the Christian era. Could it rightly be said that non-Christian Jews worshiping "the queen of heaven" during the Christian era were praying to the same monad as the Catholics when they pray to "the queen of heaven"?

An argument might be advanced that these non-Christian Jews did not believe "the queen of heaven" was the mother of Jesus, since their beliefs about her had been perpetuated unchanged from a period many centuries before Mary's Immaculate Conception; therefore, they and Catholics were not praying to the same monad; hence it would not have been reasonable for Catholics to try to enlighten these Jews (in a manner paralleling Paul's statement to the Athenians) by saying, "She whom ye ignorantly pray to we will now declare to you is the mother of Jesus."

As I have pointed out, however, persons who call a particular historical monad by a particular name often disagree about his history or character. But their disagreement does not prove they are not arguing about the same monad. In this case, the fact that certain Jews living in the Christian era prayed to "the queen of heaven," without believing her to be the mother of Jesus—as Catholics do—would not have precluded discussion between the two groups about "the queen of heaven" from being meaningful; for the title "queen of heaven" is an appellative conveying a unique function: it implies the monad so designated has not and never has had a congener in heaven.

Nevertheless, if a person in an ancient era can have the same feeling about a *conceptual* monad as another person in a later era does about a *real* monad called by the same unique appellative, does this not illustrate the fallacy inherent in the entire concept of human orientation toward real monads whose identities are unknown?

The ancient Egyptians called the goddess Isis "the queen of heaven." Therefore, the Jews in Egypt in the sixth century B.C.E. who prayed to "the queen of heaven" probably called her "Isis."

Indeed, it is probable that the nominal worship of Isis was introduced into Europe in the fourth century B.C.E. by soldiers of Alexander the Great who had conquered Egypt and then were themselves conquered by her national religion; and that when the nominal worship of Jesus was introduced into Europe, the name "Mary" was substituted for "Isis" as the name of "the queen of heaven."

There is no evidence that the early Christian missionaries who migrated from Palestine thought the mother of Jesus was the queen of heaven. The phrase "queen of heaven" does not appear in the New Testament, and appears in the Old Testament only in connection with the corrupt practices of the Jews who fled to Egypt in Jeremiah's era. The probability is that the early European converts to Christianity were reluctant to relinquish the image of a compassionate mother in heaven conveyed to them by the words "queen of heaven"; and that the inevitable conflict on this point between the missionaries from Palestine and the European converts was ultimately resolved by a compromise in which the missionaries accepted the belief in the queen of heaven and

116

the converts accepted the transference of that exalted office from Isis to Mary.

On the subject of belief in Christ, Dante wrote a verse echoing in part a passage of the New Testament:

None ever hath ascended to this realm,
Who hath not been a believer in Christ,
Either before or after the blest limbs
Were nailed upon the wood. But lo! of those
Who call "Christ, Christ," there shall be many found,
In Judgment, further off from him by far,
Than such to whom his name was never known.
Christians like these the Aethiop shall condemn.

Paradiso: Canto 19

Dante was evidently paraphrasing the following passage from the New Testament, substituting the words "Christ, Christ" for "Lord, Lord": "Not every one that saith unto me, Lord, Lord, shall enter into the kingdom of heaven; but he that doeth the will of my Father which is in heaven. Many will say to me in that day, Lord, Lord, have we not prophesied in thy name? and in thy name have cast out devils? and in thy name done many wonderful works? And then will I profess unto them, I never knew you: depart from me, ye that work iniquity" (Matthew 7:21-23).

The great poet's point obviously is that a person's belief in Christ is necessary but not sufficient for his salvation. But Dante's thinking is as fallacious as that of all Christians who place believers who never perceived Christ in the same category with those persons who lived nineteen centuries ago who actually knew him and believed him to be the Christ. Dante failed to understand the enormous difference between a person's mere belief in the history and essence of an entity unknown to him, and his ability to know him for what he is when he does know him.

117

It is meaningless to talk about Christians living centuries after the ascension of Christ as calling him "Christ." If Christ were to reappear on earth in human form and be introduced to Christians as "Christ," and they hailed him as "Christ," only then would it be correct to say that they are calling Christ "Christ."

Twin brothers brought up together as foundlings no doubt would agree they have the same antecedents. They know that a woman who has borne children is addressed by them as "Mother." But knowing that a person has been related to both of them in this manner—perhaps even knowing much about this monad—they could rightly be said to call their mother "Mother" only if they know some of her identities, and call the specific entity having these identities "Mother."

Often when two people are introduced to each other, one of them remarks: "I am happy to know you! I have heard a great deal about you!" What this person means is that he has heard a great deal about an entity having a particular name. Now that he has been introduced to the person having this name, he actually knows him.

When Christians say that Christ is their savior, what they are really saying is that an unknown person was their savior and that they call this unknown person Christ. As to those Christians who do not even know the New Testament account of the history of Christ, when they say, "Christ is our savior," they are merely speaking "words without knowledge."

Christians say the Jews who saw Jesus and did not believe him to be the Savior were nonbelievers. But did not those Jews believe in God and the coming of the Messiah, even though they did not think of the two as being one and the same monad?

Suppose you were to board a train at Grand Central Station in New York City and sit next to a man who said,

"I am Alfred E. Perlman, the president of this railroad." Let us assume this man really is Mr. Perlman. If you were to disbelieve his claim, does this mean you do not believe the New York Central has a president and that his name is Alfred E. Perlman? If you were to relate this event to me, would it be sensible for me to say, "What's the matter with you? Don't you know that Alfred E. Perlman is the president of the New York Central?" Since I have never consciously known a person by the name of Alfred E. Perlman and am not aware of his identities through a picture, nor am I familiar with his credentials, is it not likely that had I been the one to sit next to him, I also would have doubted his claim?

The problem of knowing that Jesus was the Christ, at the time he was on earth, was much more difficult than knowing Mr. Perlman to be the president of the New York Central. For one thing, Jesus charged his disciples to tell no man he was the Christ. How, then, could he expect people to know he was the Christ? Did he expect them to be detectives as competent as Sherlock Holmes?

The present-day "acceptors of Christ" do not know his identities. If Christ were to reappear on earth in fulfillment of Christian hopes, and the "acceptors of Christ" perceived his body, would they know this to be the body of Christ? Many people living today claim to be Jesus. Some of them have been placed in insane asylums. How do the "acceptors of Christ" know that not one of these claimants is indeed he?

In one of his TV lectures, Bishop Fulton J. Sheen said that God debased Himself among men because He so loved them He wanted to live and suffer with them. The Bishop tried to convey the love God manifested to men by becoming one of them by comparing Him with a shepherd who would like to become one of his sheep for a time. According to Bishop Sheen, God did not wish to be generally known as such in His human disguise. For if men discovered Jesus was in fact

119

God in the flesh, they would have been afraid to persecute him; this in turn would have thwarted God's plan of redemption through the shedding of His blood. Why then do Roman Catholics say Jesus performed miracles to prove he was God?

The New Testament relates that John the Baptist presented himself to the people of Judea as the precursor of the Lord and the messenger of the covenant whose coming had been prophesied by Malachi (Malachi 3:1), saying, "Repent ye: for the kingdom of heaven is at hand" (Matthew 3:2) ; and, "There cometh one mightier than I after me, the latchet of whose shoes I am not worthy to stoop down and unloose" (Mark 1:7). But when Jesus started to preach and perform miracles in Galilee, John knew about this only through hearsay. Uncertain that this Galilean was the "one mightier than I," he sent messengers to Jesus asking if He was that entity: "And this rumour of him [Jesus] went forth throughout all Judea, and throughout all the region round about. And the disciples of John shewed him of all these things. And John calling unto him two of his disciples sent them to Jesus, saying, Art thou he that should come? or look we for another?" (Luke 7:17-19) .

Now John's mother, Elizabeth, and Mary, mother of Jesus, were cousins (Luke 1:36). When Elizabeth was bearing John, Mary came to visit her. Elizabeth asked, "And whence is this to me, that the mother of my Lord should come to me?" (Luke 1:43). Thus, Elizabeth knew that the son Mary carried (John's cousin) was "the one" for whom all Israel was waiting. And it might be inferred from the text that even before he was born, John knew that the infant Mary carried was the "one mightier than I," for it is written that Elizabeth said: "For, lo, as soon as the voice of thy salutation sounded in mine ears, the babe [John] leaped in my womb for joy" (Luke 1:44).

Would not Dante have said that John, according to the

New Testament the precursor who boldly proclaimed to the Judeans that the Messiah would soon come, was the greatest believer in Christ? Yet, having heard of the Messiah's exploits in Galilee, John had doubts that this Galilean was "the one."

Using the information contained in the New Testament, I wish to compare the state of John's "acceptance" of Jesus, immediately before and after his meeting with this Galilean preacher.

But first let me state the conceivabilities regarding John's acceptance of Jesus before he even heard the rumors about the Galilean preacher. There are at least three:

1. John knew Jesus, his name, and that he was the "one mightier than I."
2. John knew one of his cousins was named Jesus and that he was "the one," but did not know him.
3. John knew one of his cousins was "the one," but did not know him and did not know his name.

Let us assume that at this time only one person bore the Hebrew name which has been translated "Jesus."

The text does not tell us whether or not the name of the Galilean preacher was known to John when he first heard about him. Conceivably, the rumors were simply about a man in Galilee.

For each of the three conceivabilities regarding John's acceptance of Jesus before he heard the rumors about the Galilean preacher, there are two regarding John's faith when he first heard these rumors:

1. The first conceivability: John knew Jesus, his name, that he was "the one," and that he was the Galilean preacher. The second conceivability: John knew Jesus, his name, that he was "the one," but did not know he was the Galilean preacher.

2. The first conceivability: John knew one of his cousins was named Jesus, that he was "the one," and that he was the Galilean preacher, but did not know him. The second conceivability: John knew one of his cousins was named Jesus, that he was "the one," but did not know him and did not know he was the Galilean preacher.

3. The first conceivability: John knew one of his cousins was "the one," that his name was Jesus, that he was the Galilean preacher, but did not know him. The second conceivability: John knew one of his cousins was "the one," but did not know him, did not know his name, and did not know he was the Galilean preacher.

The first conceivability of No. 1 can be discounted, for if John knew Jesus, his name, that he was "the one," and that he was the Galilean preacher, he would not have sent messengers to him asking, "Art thou he that should come?" And if we analyze the rest of the conceivabilities, we will discover that the first conceivabilities of Nos. 2 and 3 are identical.

Therefore, there are at least four conceivabilities regarding John's acceptance of Jesus after he heard the rumors about the Galilean preacher, but prior to his meeting with him.

Now let me state the conceivabilities regarding John's acceptance of Jesus after his meeting with the Galilean preacher, when no doubt he learned his name:

The second conceivability of No. 1 now becomes: John knew Jesus, his name, that he was "the one" and that he was the Galilean preacher; the identical first conceivabilities of No. 2 and No. 3 become: John knew one of his cousins was "the one," that he was named Jesus, that he was the Galilean preacher, and knew the Galilean preacher; the second conceivability of No. 2

becomes: John knew one of his cousins was named Jesus, that he was "the one," knew the Galilean preacher, and that the Galilean's name was Jesus: and the second conceivability of No. 3 becomes: John knew one of his cousins was "the one," knew the Galilean preacher and his name.

We see that these four conceivabilities are actually identical.

The foregoing analysis shows that John's orientation toward Jesus immediately after his face-to-face meeting with him was not the same as immediately before this meeting, and that the statement that John was a believer in, or acceptor of, Christ is equivocal if it refers to the period before their face-to-face meeting.

The story that, through intermediaries, John the Baptist inquired of the Galilean preacher whether he was "the one" is in fact inconsistent with the belief that John was the precursor of the appearance of that entity in Judea. For if John had known through the inspiration of the Holy Ghost—and there is no other way he could have known it—that it was his function to announce the glad tidings of the Messiah's forthcoming appearance in Judea, then, when the Messiah was preaching in Galilee, the same infallible Holy Ghost would certainly have informed him of this. Furthermore, John, who should have been able to tell everyone else that the Messiah at long last had made his appearance as a preacher and miracle worker was obliged to trust in the truthfulness, not only of the person to whom he sent the messengers, but also of the messengers themselves. How did he know the Galilean preacher was telling the truth and was not either deluded or a charlatan? Furthermore, how did he know that the messengers had spoken to the right person? So even John the Baptist—who Christians will no doubt say was one of the foremost acceptors of Christ who ever lived—had to depend on fallible men for information

123

regarding who, what and where Christ was, and consequently could easily have been misled into accepting a false Christ.

If the assertion that John the Baptist was a believer in Jesus before meeting the Galilean preacher is equivocal, what of those Christians who never knew Christ—those believers in Christ "after the blest limbs were nailed upon the wood" of Dante's day? Or such persons as our contemporary evangelical mountebank, Rev. Dr. Graham, who exhorts his audiences "to receive Christ in your heart as your personal savior"?

Does "Receive Christ!" mean that you should imbibe Christ's spirit-essence into your own? Or that you should believe in the truth of the history of the entity called Jesus as it is reported in the New Testament? Or that you should know Christ?

If Dr. Graham is talking about the spirit-essence of Christ, is it not just as beneficial to receive Jehovah's spirit-essence, since Christ's and Jehovah's spirit-essences are consubstantial? If Graham means you should know Christ, how do you know an entity seated in heaven at the right hand of Jehovah? As to believing the New Testament's account of the life of Jesus, Dr. Graham does not think of this as a necessary concomitant to the receiving of Christ, for he exhorts his audiences to "make a decision for Christ" without further ado. He actually does not know whether his audiences are conversant with the New Testament.

Many professed believers in Christ born during the many centuries following his ascension have thought that their receiving of him did not necessarily entail knowing his identities or even much of his history, but only knowing that a man called Jesus was crucified for the sins of the world. But it is historical that the Romans crucified many who claimed to be the Messiah. Which was Jesus? I have already analyzed the notion that John the Baptist was an acceptor of Jesus and shown that the whole notion of belief in a monad is ambiguous unless the monad is known to the believer

124

through its conjunction with a body. For allegedly John the Baptist believed in Jesus before he met the Galilean preacher, yet did not know this preacher he heard so much about was "the one" he believed in.

Knowing a name is not the same as knowing the monad or entity having that name, as was illustrated in the hypothetical story about Alfred E. Perlman. Similarly, the so-called receiving, or accepting, of Jesus Christ by the present-day Christians is nothing more than the apotheosis of a name and a title.

The New Testament quotes Jesus as saying, "No man cometh unto the Father, but by me" (John 14:6). Since the Father and the Son are consubstantial in spirit-essence, this statement can be meaningful only if "me" pertains to the Son's body. It certainly does not mean that people should pray to Jesus, who commanded them to pray directly to "Our Father" (Matthew 6:9) ; nor did he ever tell anyone to pray to him to intercede with the Father.

Some Christians believe that the bread and wine in the Sacrament of the Holy Eucharist are actually the body and blood of Jesus and that one communes with Jesus by partaking of this food and drink.[1] But communing with Jesus in this way does not entail knowing his identities, any more than drinking milk entails knowing the cow that gave the milk; for the body and blood of Jesus in the form of bread and wine can in no way be distinguished from ordinary bread and wine.

Let us assume that Jesus did command his disciples to eat

[1] The command to drink blood must have been of non-Jewish origin. For no devout Jew would ever tell another to drink blood. Partaking of blood was prohibited by the Mosaic law: "Ye shall not eat of the blood" (Leviticus 19:26). The Jews have always thought of drinking blood as an extremely abhorrent practice: "And whatsoever man there be of the house of Israel, or of the strangers that sojourn among them, that eateth any manner of blood, I will set My face against that soul that eateth any manner of blood, and will cut him off from among his people" (Leviticus 17:10). The very thought of drinking blood is enough to induce revulsion in a person brought up in the Jewish faith.

his body and drink his blood "in remembrance of me" (1 Corinthians 11:24-26). On a previous occasion he had said, "For the poor always ye have with you; but me ye have not always" (John 12:8). But when he was about to ascend to heaven he said to his disciples: "Lo, I am with you always, even unto the end of the world" (Matthew 28:20). If Jesus promised his disciples that he would be with them always, why did he say, "but me ye have not always"? Why did he command them to drink his blood and eat his body "in remembrance of me"? Again, the only possible answer is that "me" means the body in which he appeared to men. But only those who knew Jesus' body could have remembered it. Therefore, the communion in remembrance of Jesus could have been efficacious only when it was performed by those followers who knew him in his human manifestation. Why then do present-day Christians perform communion in remembrance of identities they cannot possibly remember, having never perceived them?

The Docetae, a Christian sect of the first and second centuries, maintained that Jesus' body was a phantom. This sect was condemned as heretical. Nevertheless, present-day Christians commonly believe that Jesus was resurrected in a "glorified body," not the body in which he first appeared on earth. If this be true, which of the bodies is in the wafer of unleavened bread? Is the blood which is drunk the same which was shed for the sins of the world, or newly created blood? And is this blood miraculously transfused into the wine from the body of Jesus presently seated at the right hand of the Father in heaven?

Chapter 10

"HIS OWN RECEIVED HIM NOT"

What do Christians mean when they say, "He came unto his own, and his own received him not"? (John 1:11). Who were "his own"? Were they the people of his home town of Nazareth? his family? or all the people living in Palestine at the time Jesus was on earth?

Most Christians will say that the Jews, having been God's chosen people, were "his own": therefore they were the ones who "received him not." Probably no scriptural words have been more often quoted by the Christian clergy to inspire hatred of the Jews than "his own received him not."

The word "Jew" is a transliteration of a Hebrew word. It does not appear in any Biblical work written before the civil war between the tribes of southern and northern Palestine, which resulted in the creation of two nations, "Judah" and "Samaria." Judah was so named because the majority of its constituents were of the tribe of Judah. The word "Jew" is derived from "Judah," and originally meant a descendant of Israel who was of the Kingdom of Judah.

The people of Judah, the Kingdom of the South, came to think of the Samarians as "the lost ten tribes," not only because of the political and religious schism but also because many invasions of Samaria depleted the populace. Nevertheless, the New Testament refers to Samarians (Samaritans) and Samarian cities existing as late as the time of Jesus' ministry in Palestine, as well as to the great antagonism which still existed between them and the Jewish community.

Many books written by partisans of Judah during the existence of Samaria have come down to us as sacred scripture. The Samaritans also had their sacred books, but none written from their point of view have been incorporated into the canon of books called "the Bible."

The great majority of the children of Israel dispersed in the countries of Europe in the Christian era were of the Kingdom of Judah. The few Samaritans who migrated to Europe were forced to merge with their Jewish enemies because of the greater enmity of the Gentiles, which resulted in the dissolution in Europe of the Samaritan community. Thus, in modern usage "the Jews" generally means the children of Israel and persons who either have become part of this group through conversion or are descended from converted persons; and the entire history of the children of Israel from the time of the patriarchs is today known as "The History of the Jews." But since none of the children of Israel who lived before the schism of the tribes were called Jews it is also customary to refer to that ancient people as Israelites.

In Christendom, the Jews as a group are physically distinguishable from other groups; certain physical traits predominate among Jews. When people see a picture in a newspaper of a gathering of Jews, they usually know this is a Jewish group. The pronounced physical resemblance between many Jews and certain leaders of Middle Eastern states such as Kings Feisal, Abdullah and Ibn Saud indicates that present-day Jews in the Diaspora of Christendom are still preponderantly of Semitic stock. Of course, in the Middle East live millions of Semites other than Jews. If millions of Arabs had migrated to America and Europe, the antagonism to Jews, so widespread in these continents, could not properly be termed anti-Semitism. Certainly the antagonism of the Arabs of the Middle East toward their Jewish neighbors cannot be termed anti-Semitism. On the contrary, the **Arabs** think of themselves as being the true Semites, regarding the Jewish immigrants to the Middle East as being only partly Semitic because of their assimilation of European physical traits.

Indeed, there are many Jews who resemble Gentiles of European extraction, indicating that one or more of their forebears have become Jews through intermarriage, illegitimate union or religious conversion.

Persons who formerly practiced the Jewish religion but no longer do so, and those whose forebears were converted to another religion, are in many instances thought of as Jews. Paul thought of himself as a Jew even after his conversion to Christianity: "Hath God cast away his people? God forbid. For I also am a Jew" (Romans 11:1). Certainly in Christendom a person who is ethnically Semitic is thought of as a Jew, even if he does not practice the Jewish religion. The case of Senator Goldwater illustrates this.

The case of composer Richard Wagner is another example. He was born into and brought up by a Christian family. In his early days, however, when his enemies were legion, he was often caricatured in the German press as a Jew with a hook nose. Indeed, although the caricatures exaggerated it, he did have a Semitic nose; and after his death, investigation revealed he was the natural son of one Ludwig Geyer, a Jewish actor. Geyer, a friend of the Wagner family, married Richard's mother after the elder Wagner's death, becoming young Richard's legal stepfather. The principal facts proving that Geyer sired Richard are that the two bore a striking resemblance, and that the younger Wagner looked nothing like the elder Wagner, a police official having no artistic talent.

The irony of Wagner's Jewish extraction is that he became a great antagonist of the Jews of Germany, abhorring them as foreigners and Christ-killers. Psychologically, it is likely that this antagonism stemmed from the fact that his legal stepfather (actually his natural father) was Jewish. During the Nazi period, books on the subject of Wagner's true extraction were suppressed in Germany, for Hitler was a great admirer of Wagner, considering him to be the quintessence of the genius of the Aryan race.

During the Roman overlordship of Palestine, the country was divided into provinces, one called "Judea," another "Galilee." According to our present-day interpretation of the word "Jew," the people of Nazareth in the province of Galilee were Jews. They had a synagogue, adhered to the ancient faith of Israel, and during certain holidays even went to Jerusalem in Judea to worship with the Judeans: "Then when he was come unto Galilee, the Galileans received him, having seen all the things that he did at Jerusalem at the feast: for *they also* went unto the feast" (John 4:45) .[1]

Today, no one thinks of Jews as people necessarily residing within the confines of definite physical boundaries. But in contrast to our present-day definition of Jews, at least one of the authors of the Gospel of John thought of the word "Jews" as meaning only the indigenous populace of the province of Judea. To that author none of the Galileans were Jews. Several passages in this Gospel illustrate this. For example: "After these things Jesus walked in Galilee: for he would not walk in Jewry, because the Jews sought to kill him" (John 7:1); "Then after that saith he to his disciples, Let us go unto Judea again. His disciples say unto him, Master, the Jews of late sought to stone thee; and goest thou thither again?" (John 11: 7-8) .

Was Jesus a masochistic daredevil looking for trouble? At one time he went from Judea to Galilee because "the Jews sought to kill him." Later, against the advice of his disciples, he decided to return to Judea. Evidently he was suddenly possessed by the irresistible urge to put his head in the lion's mouth. Moreover, according to Christian theology, Jesus

[1] Italics mine.

130

came to die for the sins of the world. Why then did he flee from a place where the people sought to kill him?

It is not at all clear from the text of the Gospel of John that the author of the words "his own" was referring to the people we would call Jews. Verses 1:10-11 read: "He was in the world, and the world was made by him, and the world knew him not. He came unto his own, and his own received him not." Could not "his own received him not" mean that the world received him not?

However, in the Gospel of Matthew the words "his own country" mean the town of Nazareth, where Jesus' family resided from his childhood on, as shown by the following quotation: "And when he was come into his own country,[2] he taught them in their synagogues, insomuch that they were astonished, and said, 'Whence hath this man this wisdom and these mighty works? Is not this the carpenter's son? Is not his mother called Mary? And his brethren, James, and Joses, and Simon, and Judas? And his sisters, are they not all with us? Whence then hath this man all these things?' And they were offended in him. But Jesus said unto them, A prophet is not without honour save in his own country, and in his own house" (Matthew 13:54-57).

In the Gospel of Luke's account of this same event: "And all they in the synagogue, when they heard these things, were filled with wrath, and rose up and thrust him out of the city (4:28-29).

But the author who wrote "Then when he was come into Galilee, the Galileans received him" (John 4:45) could not have been referring to the people of Nazareth, who "thrust him out of the city." Yet was not Nazareth in Galilee?

A fallacy one notices time and again in the New Testament is the general statement which contradicts a particularization. One finds statements that *"the* Jews" did so-and-so

[2] "Country" here must mean the town of Nazareth, since Jesus never left Palestine when he was on earth.

131

or "*the* Galileans" did such-and-such, and contradictory statements about particular Jews or Galileans.

If the author of "He came unto his own and his own received him not" was referring to a particular group of people, not "the world," he should have been explicit and named that people. Assuming he was referring to a particular people, was their refusal to receive Jesus collective, such as the American people's collective rejection of Nixon in the presidential election, even though nearly half of them voted for him? It is plain that no matter whom he meant by "his own," the author must have meant a collective refusal to receive "him," for the verse immediately following says that many did receive him: "But as many as received him, to them gave he power to become the sons of God" (John 1:27). But according to modern Christian theology, is not the receiving of Christ properly a matter of individual prerogative? Why should a Christian author write about a collective nonreceiving of Christ?

Let us assume that by the words "his own" the author of John 1:11 meant "the Jews" and that the words "the Jews" meant the same to him as to us in the twentieth century. He could not have been referring to the hundreds of thousands of Jews who at the time of Jesus' ministry were living in cities such as Alexandria and Damascus, which were not even in Palestine. Certainly Jesus did not come "unto his own" in Alexandria and Damascus. Furthermore, since Josephus Flavius, who lived in Palestine shortly after the time of Jesus, did not mention him in his monumental historical books, evidently he was not even well known in Palestine. Therefore, the author of John 1:11 would have expressed himself more accurately had he said, "He came to some of his own; of those of his own to whom he came, some received him and others received him not." In this way, he would have avoided casting aspersions on an entire people. But perhaps it was his purpose to deprecate the Jews.

132

Moreover, assuming "his own" were the Jews, it is not clear from the text of the fourth Gospel precisely what the words "received him not" actually meant to their author. Did he mean the Jews did not believe Jesus was the Messiah? Or that they did not wish to associate with him? Or did the author mean they did not admit him to their temples? Or that they did not believe the doctrines he propounded?

Almost everyone has had the experience of receiving guests without knowing who they were. Certainly Jesus was received into many Jewish homes and temples. However, Christians generally consider the words "his own received him not" to mean that the Jews did not know he was the Messiah. But if the Christians think "the Galileans received him" (John 4:45) means that the Galileans (who were Jews, in our modern definition of the word) were hospitable to Jesus without knowing he was the Messiah, why should they interpret the words "received him not" (John 1:11) to mean that the Jews did not know who he was? Should they not be consistent in their interpretation of the word "received"?

According to Christians, the difference between the "rejector of Christ" during Christ's time on earth and the "receiver of Christ" of today is that the "rejector of Christ" knew him but did not believe him to be the Messiah, whereas the "receiver of Christ" believes him to be the Messiah without knowing him. But belief and unbelief are not properly contrasted in this manner, for in one case belief is contingent on the ability to identify; in the other case it is not. The "receivers" of Christ are not greater believers than the people who "received him not," for the latter also believed in the Messiah, even though they could not identify him as such.

Chapter 11

MAN'S LOVE

A man's love for anything which is only physical, such as the Grand Canyon, depends on his having seen either the thing itself or a reproduction of it. However, if his impression of the object has become so distorted from his original perception of it that he will no longer be able to recognize it should he see it again, it cannot be correctly said that he loves the thing as it is.

Is it possible for one to love a monad which has been joined with an animate body if he does not know any of its identities? Such an emotional orientation, I maintain, is as impossible as is the love of the Grand Canyon by a person who has never seen it or a reproduction of it. For example, you owe a great deal to your great-great-grandmother, for you are one of her "footprints on the sands of time." Perhaps you have been taught from early childhood to love her, and, having discovered her diary, learned much about her. Consequently, you experience a feeling of pleasure—which you probably call love—whenever your great-great-grandmother is mentioned. But if you have never met this progenitor of yours and have never seen her picture, is not your "love" for her actually a conditioned mental reflex? If you were to discover in your attic a picture of her and not know this is her picture, is it not possible you might ask, "Who could love a woman with a face like this?" So we see that you are in no way emotionally oriented toward this entity whom you know a great deal about but have never known. And since you are not oriented toward this entity you certainly are not oriented toward the monad which was a component of this entity.

The knowledge you may have that an existing person is related to you in a particular way is not in itself sufficient to orient you toward him. For example, it is known that women who have given birth in hospitals have gone home with the wrong babies and loved them as though they were their own. Such a woman does not actually love her own baby, although she thinks she does.

It is said that a child instinctively loves its mother. But does not this love spring from the child's gratitude toward the person continually caring for it? The fact that in most cases the latter is the child's mother does not prove that a child instinctively loves its mother.

When one knows someone has done something for him, he cannot feel gratitude toward him for this particular deed unless he knows him and is aware that this particular person is his benefactor. In Dickens' *Great Expectations*, a blacksmith's apprentice is aided by a benefactor to become an elegant gentleman in London. For many years this man does not know who his benefactor is. When at long last the benefactor visits the former blacksmith's apprentice, it turns out he is an escaped convict to whom he once gave food and drink. Before this meeting he had thought that his benefactor was an eccentric old woman of his acquaintance, and had directed his feelings of gratitude toward her. In this illustration of gratitude felt toward the wrong entity, the benefited actually knew his benefactor, but felt no gratitude toward him, even though he did have a feeling of gratitude. How then can one feel gratitude toward an entity he does not know at all, no matter what this entity may have done for him?

Similarly, it is impossible for one to hate someone who has done him an injury if he does not know him. In recent years we have heard much about "faceless informers." Suppose a faceless informer slandered you. Even if you know this person you cannot hate him for this particular offense, since you do not know which of the persons you know is the informer. How then could you hate someone who has done you an injury if you do not know him at all?

It has thus been shown that in order for one to be oriented in any way toward a monad—through love, hatred or otherwise—it is necessary for him to know that monad through perceiving a body with which that monad has been joined. Thus, when one avers his love for some worthy historical personage whom he has never known—either through seeing his identities or a reproduction of them—should he not rather say that this person was *worthy* of being loved by those who did know him?

Let us assume that the monad joined with the body of Jesus was in fact the Son of God, one of the "persons" of the Triune Godhead. The entity is no longer on earth, for it has ascended to heaven; its identities have not been known on earth for almost two thousand years. Thus, so far as we on earth are concerned, this human body is as defunct as if it had been cremated after its crucifixion: "Wherefore henceforth know we no man after the flesh; yea, though we have known Christ after the flesh, yet now henceforth know we him no more" (2 Corinthians 5:16). Even if this entity now sits at the right hand of the Father in heaven, so far as we are concerned, his physical existence in the cosmos has no more function or utility than a small stone in the outer reaches of Siberia. And since the Son of God-monad exists throughout eternity, it is meaningless to think of him as being perpetually joined with a human body no longer performing any earthly functions.

The statement that Christ sits at the right hand of the Father is not factually significant, for if he were *standing* at the right hand of the Father or even if the Father had no right hand, what difference would it make? If we do not perceive this body, of what significance is its posture?

It would be possible for us to love the Son of God-monad in his conjunction with the body of Jesus if we had a genuine reproduction of his physical features. But since the many representations of him were made by artists who had not the vaguest notion of how he looked, what the beholder really loves is not the entity Jesus but the artist's conception of him. Thus, even if you believe Jesus redeemed you by his sacrifice on the cross, and even if you know his entire history, you cannot love him. Your great-great-grandmother did much for you—you would not be here if it were not for her —yet, not knowing what she looked like, you do not love her.

Pascal is reputed to have said, "The entire religion of the Jews consists of the love of God." This statement is senseless. It is beyond man's mental capacity to obey the commandment of Deuteronomy 11:1—"Thou shalt love the Lord thy God" (assuming "the Lord" here refers to God and that "God" is a correct translation). The writer of the statement, "If a man say I love God, and hateth his brother, he is a liar: for he that loveth not his brother, whom he hath seen, how can he love God whom he hath not seen?" (1 John 4:20), indicates he understood that knowing a monad's identities is a prerequisite to loving it. But he failed to develop this thought to its logical conclusion—that even if you love a brother whom you have seen, you cannot love God, for you have not see Him.

Now if the ancient Israelites had believed "the Lord" (Jehovah) to be purely a spirit, the commandment "Thou shalt love the Lord thy God" would have been salutary in a negative way—by its implicit prohibition of the worship of idols. However, as I have said, the ancient Palestine Israelites believed the brass serpent made by Moses in the wilderness was Jehovah. But when at long last the Israelites came to believe that the "I" (or "Me") of the first commandment was purely a spirit having no identities, they could only know who "I" was *not*, not who "I" *was*. When you read Deuteronomy 5:6-7—"I am the Lord your God. . . . Thou shalt have no other gods before Me"—you are reading about a spirit-monad who is quoted by Moses as having said "I." How do you distinguish this monad from another unidentifiable monad, also calling himself "I," who might address you through an interlocutor?

Suppose a person who has never seen his brother but knows his name is John, receives a letter saying, "I am your long lost brother John. Don't think anyone else is your brother." Is any meaning conveyed by the word "I" in this letter, unless a photograph or some other means of identification is enclosed with it? So far as you are concerned, "I" could be almost anyone.

And who is the "I" of the New Testament verse, "I am the way and the truth and the life: no man cometh unto the Father, but by me"? (John 14:6). The Trinitarian Christians officially believe the "I" of this verse and the "I" of "I am the Lord your God" are consubstantial monads, but that the "I" of the New Testament became a component of a human entity. If this is so, it is meaningless to say that no man can come to one "I" except through the other "I", unless the latter is identifiable. Therefore, only those who knew "the way, the truth and the life" in the flesh could come to the Father (whatever coming to the Father may mean).

Perhaps the psychological reason Christians are unable to understand Judaism is that it is inconceivable to them that God can be loved if He is invisible. In this belief they are

138

right. But evidently they think this problem was solved by God manifesting Himself in the person of Jesus. Since, however, this entity has been in heaven seated at the right hand of the Father for more than nineteen centuries, the Christians' professed love for Jesus is as unreal as the Jews' love for Jehovah.

If, however, the entity Jesus was really God in the flesh, possibly many people loved God without knowing Him to be God, for people love many entities without knowing what they are in their spirit-essences.

How many people there are who go about saying Jesus is their savior, not knowing what "savior" means, for they do not know what they are being saved from! And even if it is assumed that everybody knows what "savior" means, they only know that their savior is called Jesus. They do not know Jesus' human identities from other identities. To say you believe a human entity designated by a particular name is your savior is meaningless if you do not know the human entity you say is your savior. If Christians counter this argument with the assertion that Jesus in his spirit-essence, not his human form, is their savior, they are being even more ridiculous than those who say the body of Jesus was their savior. For it is certainly not possible for one to know a spirit designated by one name from another spirit designated by another name. Since all spirits are unidentifiable, one cannot know which spirit is designated by a particular name.

All we can know about defunct historical entities whose identities are unknown is their names and their "footprints on the sands of time." Saying we love the entities is like saying that since we love the footprints we necessarily love the feet.

It is very easy for a preacher to tell people to love God and hate the devil, but all this preacher can really do is expound the difference between their "footprints." It is possible to love one set of footprints and hate the other, but not to love

God and hate the devil.

The New Testament says, "By their fruits ye shall know them" (Matthew 7:20). No doubt this means you learn about people's characters and abilities from the things they do. But can you know a man is an architect by observing and admiring a building he has designed if you do not know him? Or if knowing him, you do not know he is the designer of the building? If you pluck apples off a tree, you know it is an apple tree. But when you buy an apple in a store, you do not know which tree produced it; in short, you do not know the identities or location of the tree by knowing its fruit. To say you love a tree which produced a good apple and hate a tree which produced a bad apple is meaningless, unless you have seen the apples as they were plucked off the trees. Likewise, to say you love a historical entity simply because you know the good "fruits" he produced is meaningless if you do not know him through identity.

The statement "By their fruits ye shall know them" is not necessarily true even when you know that a person of your acquaintance has produced certain "fruits." For example, a person not charitable by nature may perform charitable acts out of ulterior motives. Often men give to charity with different motives in mind. Some people are honest because it is their nature to be honest, others because "honesty is the best policy." So we see one does not always know what people are by their "fruits."

Teaching people to love a particular entity none of whose identities are known by them is like teaching children born blind to love a flag. For these blind children to love this flag they must have perceived it as such. Of course, by means of touch it is possible for them to love a piece of cloth manufactured as a flag. But a flag consists of a configuration of colors, not of the material which conveys this configuration. The same material can be used to make things other than this flag, and many materials can be used to convey its

140

color configuration. So the blind child's love for the material which conveys this flag's color configuration is not tantamount to loving the flag as such. Even if a braille system exists for conveying to the blind the relative positions of the various stars and stripes of the American flag, it cannot convey the colors themselves.

One might teach a deaf person who has never heard Bach's music to say that Bach was a musical genius. It is even conceivable that such a person could expound with great erudition on the subject of Bach's musical genius, having learned this subject by rote. He may even think he loves Bach's music. But this "love" is really only a conditioned mental reflex, certainly not elicited by his knowledge or understanding of Bach's genius.

Another illustration of "words without knowledge": one who teaches a child to say Napoleon was a military genius is in reality teaching this child nothing about the essence of Napoleon as a military man in contradistinction to the essences of other military men not military geniuses. One must not only understand military affairs in general, but also know something about the details of Napoleon's campaigns to appreciate his military genius. How many people there are in this world who say they admire Napoleon who have only a dim notion of what they admire!

Some Christians say that to love God is nothing more nor less than to do His will: "For this is the love of God, that we keep his commandments" (1 John 5:3). If this be true, then even an atheist can love God, for it is possible for him to do God's will without believing God willed it. It is more than probable there are many atheists belonging to churches who hypocritically do God's will as interpreted by their clergymen because of the goodwill this brings them in the community.

Spinoza, believing the universe to be God by extension, defined the love of God as the knowledge of the universe:

"We have greater and more perfect knowledge of God in proportion to our knowledge of natural phenomena: conversely, since the knowledge of an effect through its cause is the same thing as the knowledge of a particular property of a cause, the greater our knowledge of natural phenomena, the more perfect is our knowledge of the essence of God, which is the cause of all things." "All things which are, are in God and must be conceived through Him and therefore He is the cause of all things which are in Himself. Moreover, outside of God there can be no substance, that is to say outside of Him nothing can exist which is in itself."

If one accepts Spinoza's notion of the love of God, the scientist, not the theist, is the greatest lover of God, even though, paradoxically, some scientists profess to be atheists. Moreover, if man is part of God, then man's love of himself is also the love of God. According to Spinoza, then, we cannot love anything but God, for He is immanent, not transcendent, in all things—all things are in Him. Spinoza, in effect, proves God exists by defining that which exists as God.

"Love" is, in fact, one of the most ambiguous words in present-day usage. It is used to connote sexual passion and conjugal union; one's affection for an object and the object of one's affection; self-abnegation and lechery; and the sentiment of goodwill and devotion. Some interpretations of "love" involve physical action; others merely acts of the mind. Love is generally considered an honorable and commendable thing, but when it is thought of as carnal desire—even between people married to each other—it is often alternately referred to by the very same person as good and bad; degrading and noble; gentle and violent; pure and dirty.

"Love" is used to mean a man's devotion to a woman for her character and also the emotion he may feel toward her as an example of physical womanhood—a "thought of nature," as Schopenhauer puts it. This latter type of love is like the love of music. One does not sympathize with or feel compassion toward music itself, for music has no feelings or thoughts of its own. Although women do have thoughts and feelings of their own, there can be no doubt that man's love for his mate, in one sense of the word, is completely selfish and physical, as expressed in the "Song of Songs"— probably the last word in sensualism without sentiment—in which the beloved is seen as a physical phenomenon rather than as a personality. On the other hand, there is platonic love, in which one feels compassion, affection and sympathy for a woman, as expressed in Scott's *Lay of the Last Minstrel:*

> True love's the gift which God has
>   given
> To man alone beneath the heaven:
>   It is not fantasy's hot fire,
>   Whose wishes, soon as granted,
>   fly;
> It liveth not in fierce desire,
>   With dead desire it doth not die;
> It is the secret sympathy,
> The silver link, the silken tie,
> Which heart to heart, and mind to
>   mind,
> In body and in soul can bind.

Often sexual passion is not a manifestation of affection. It is rather sexual passion which spurs some persons to advance false protestations of undying affection as a moral excuse for gratifying carnal desire. That in many cases this is true is evidenced by the fact that many pre-adolescent boys show no affection for girls, indeed deny having this feeling. But when these boys mature physically, suddenly they make a complete turnabout in their attitude toward girls. This

143

indicates that their "love" is based not on heartfelt affection but on physical need.

In *The Kreutzer Sonata* Tolstoy treats the question of sexual passion in marriage when based solely on physical need. The novel, probably a reflection of Tolstoy's own unhappy marriage, reveals the savage mutual hatred which this interdependence can arouse.

The human libido, both in and out of marriage, can be aroused by any of a multitude of thoughts which have no connection with the affections. For example, rape is a crime of sexual passion, often precipitated by a morbid fascination to terrorize and by the thrill derived from contemplating a sadistic act. If a man is brought up in repressive circumstances, he might well become a sadist, a masochist or a rapist. There are even some kinds of sexual passion in which there is no desire for contact with another person. Fetishism, for example, is the carnal fascination of embracing some kind of garment.

In every human mind, coursing like a complex of interconnected rivers and tributaries, are many dormant thoughts, each a potential master of the libido. We all have these thoughts, just as we all have jugular veins and livers. The volume and flow of these rivers, however, are controlled by mental conditioning. If a particular river becomes swollen and overflows its banks, thereby inundating the entire mind, this river—this particular carnal thought—masters the libido. One's carnal behavior is greatly influenced by his background. At different stages of a man's life, his sexual behavior may change because of changed external circumstances. If at a particular juncture in his life his mind has become conditioned to a fascination for darkness and the unknown, he is apt to be drawn to the night, which would probably cause him to select a dark-haired, dark-eyed woman for a wife or paramour. If at another juncture in his life he should become fascinated by light and openness, he would

144

probably choose a blond woman for a mate. The point is that this man's behavior is a result not only of his temperament, but of external influences which may in turn swell one, then another of the carnal rivers of his mind.

A prison psychiatrist, by observing a sex offender's word patterns and facial reactions, tries to deduce clues as to the conditioning influences that have led this unfortunate person off the beaten track of social decorum. Then, by subtle suggestion, he tries to gradually augment the salutary rivers of his mind—that is, to recondition him to behave in a manner acceptable to society.

But even though it is possible for a psychiatrist to redirect a person's affections by suggestion, affection itself is deeply subjective and cannot be imposed by anything extrinsic to the mind itself. One cannot instill affection into persons not affectionate by nature; and even in those affectionate by nature it is impossible for them by conscious volition to summon their powers of affection. The Gospel of John implies that Jesus himself was able to love only one of his twelve disciples. "The disciple whom Jesus loved" is mentioned in this Gospel at least four times. Moreover, Simon Peter, whom the Roman Catholics believe was the first pope, was not this disciple, as the following verses indicate: "Therefore that disciple whom Jesus loved saith unto Peter, it is the Lord" (21:7); "Then Peter, turning about, seeth the disciple whom Jesus loved following" (21:20).

In the Old Testament commandment, "Thou shalt love thy neighbor as thyself" (Leviticus 19:18), which Jesus reiterated (Matthew 19:19), the notion is implicit that it is possible for a person to love *every* kind of person, for anyone is potentially a neighbor. Yet Jesus was able to love only one of his disciples.

How, then, could he have been a lover of mankind?

Chapter 12

AN ALLEGORY OF TIME AND A CLOCK

Let me illustrate through an allegory the absurdities inherent in the Christian notion of man's relation to God—his understanding of His essence and his knowledge and love of Him through Jesus.

Let us go back to the early days of the marvelous invention which rotates its hands through equal angles for equal periods of time—the clock. Suppose the first man who succeeded in constructing such a mechanism was a seafarer who traded it for a pearl on a primitive, remote island.

While the clock was on the island, the great majority of the natives did not even hear about it, and only a few were privileged to see it. Of those who saw the clock, some were told it was an indicator of time; others, not being told of this fact, admired and loved it for its ticking, not understanding the significance of this sound. Of those who saw the clock and were told of its function as an indicator of time, some believed in its efficacy and others were doubtful, until it became a bitter source of contention, engendering two opposing factions. Eventually the nonbelievers succeeded in gaining possession of the clock and destroyed it.

After the clock's destruction, the debate continued, so that for many generations people on the island heard of the controversy and were converted to one or the other faction.

The believers, who were told the mechanism's name was "clock," claimed their belief in "clock" was equal to that of the original believers who had actually seen it, and they continually railed not only against the original nonbelievers who had seen the clock but also against their nonbelieving contemporaries. Such great hatred was aroused against nonbelievers that violent persecution followed, countless people being tortured and put to death.

One can understand that while the clock was on the island those who had seen it and believed in its efficacy as an indicator of time would resent the nay-sayers who saw it and denied its utility. But how could a believer, in retrospect, expect those who had seen the clock but were not told of its function to deduce the clock was an indicator of time? And what of the great preponderance of people living on the island at the time the clock was there who did not even hear of it?

And how does the believer living many generations after the clock's destruction, never having seen it and having no notion of what it looked like, know that if he were to see a picture of the clock he would know what it represents? In what way is this "believer" a greater believer in the clock than those living on the island while the clock was there who did not believe in its efficacy?

As to the understanding of time, what real distinction is there between believer and nonbeliever? Certainly, a person's belief in the onetime existence of a clock is no criterion for his understanding of time: a nonbeliever can understand time as well as a believer. Kant believed time was merely a subjective form of human thought, having no objective existence. Perhaps this is true. But the concept of time must have been understood by most people in a practical sense, if not in a relativistic sense, before the first clock was invented; otherwise it would never have been invented.

Let us assume Christians are right in their assertion that Jesus was God incarnate as a man. If we think of God,

147

Jesus (His physical indicator), and the world as time, clock, and island respectively, we see, first, that belief in Jesus, either during or after his appearance as an entity on earth, has nothing to do with belief in God; second, that belief in Jesus has nothing to do with the understanding of God's essence; third, that many who saw Jesus may have loved him, without knowing him to be the human incarnation of God, but that all who presently say they love Jesus do not love him, for they know only his name, not him; fourth, that God's manifestation as Jesus, far from bringing peace on earth, has been a source of much needless misunderstanding and strife among men.

Chapter 13

INSTITUTIONS AND ATTITUDES

a) *The Communist Party*

Every organization—whether it be political, religious or business—must have its rules and regulations. Some organizations, particularly religious ones, also have a system of tenets which members are obligated to believe in. At the head of every organization are officers who formulate and are responsible for its policies. For example, in a recent U.S. antitrust case, several manufacturing companies were found guilty, and certain officers were held responsible for the actions of their company as a whole. It is often true that the majority of an organization's rank-and-file members are not completely familiar with its policies or tenets; but when the governing body's authority to formulate them is no longer accepted by the rank and file, the organization as such can no longer function.

The members of Christian organizations profess to believe in the tenets of the Bible. But many are either partly or wholly ignorant of its contents. Thus, it does not follow that when one believes in a book he necessarily believes it.

However, it is true that you may believe either part or all

149

of a book's contents without having read it or heard it quoted. In such a case, you believe certain things without being aware they are propounded as truths by this book.

That membership in a religious organization having an official canon does not necessarily bind one in a commonality of belief is illustrated by a survey conducted by a certain Dr. Yashio Fukuyama, reported in the *New York Times,* January 8, 1961. The survey encompassed more than four thousand members of twelve Congregational churches in North-Central and Northeastern states. Dr. Fukuyama concluded that members of the Congregational Church could be categorized as: (1) the religiously knowledgeable church member; (2) the organizational member; (3) the unquestioning believer; (4) the inward experiencing, devotional member; (5) the "nominal" members comprising 33 percent of the membership and not belonging to any of the other four categories.

Moreover, we are all unwitting promulgators of doctrines and notions whose sources we are unaware of. It is often unfair to charge persons with being collaborators with religious or political organizations unless these persons so proclaim themselves. For example, it is not fair to call an anti-Semite a Nazi, simply because the Nazis were persecutors of the Jews, for there are many who agreed with part of Hitler's program, yet opposed Nazi domination of the world. Stigmatizing one as a Nazi, Catholic, Protestant, Marxist or Communist, to name a few labels, simply because he agrees with some of the opinions held by others who do stigmatize themselves with such a label, is what I call *nominism.* Nominism is also the boundless propensity of mankind to have violent emotions about creeds, political, social or religious, and toward persons openly espousing such creeds, without having a thorough knowledge of these creeds. My purpose is to name a folly probably universal in mankind, not to stigmatize anyone as a nominist.

Marxism, unlike Communism, cannot properly be characterized as an institutional movement; it is, rather, attitudinal. The Communist Party has, of course, canonized the writings of Karl Marx as its holy writ. But several organizations not affiliated with the Communist Party—some, indeed, violently antagonistic to it—have canonized the writings of Marx as being infallible; each avers that it alone is the true inheritor of the Marxist legacy. Trotskyites and Communists, both of whom call themselves "Marxist," think of each other as the devil quoting scripture for his own ends. To the Communists there is no epithet more derogatory than "Trotskyite." And there are many who consider themselves Marxists who do not belong to any organization which calls itself Marxist.

One of the great troubles with "anti-Communism" in America is the noministic confounding of Communism with Marxism, because of the well-known belief of the Communists that Marx was the progenitor of their party and the Russian Revolution. To many, Marxism and Communism are synonymous because the Communist Party claims that, through an apostolic succession of leaders initiated by Marx himself, it is the only legitimate heir of the Marxist legacy.

The question of which individuals were the progenitors of mass movements is a very complicated one; one ought to differentiate between progenitors-by-intent and progenitors-through-misinterpretation. Does anyone believe Jesus was the progenitor-by-intent of the Spanish Inquisition simply because the inquisitors claimed they derived legitimate authority through their rank in the church he had founded? Moreover, is it plausible the protagonist of the New Testament was the progenitor-by-intent of a universal faith, through his posthumous investiture with that exalted office by Paul—the apostle who was not even one of the original disciples and was ignorant of Jesus' command to his disciples to "go not unto the way of the Gentiles, and into any city of the Samaritans enter ye not: But go rather to the lost sheep of the house of Israel"? (Matthew 10:5-6).

Marx was certainly not the progenitor-by-intent of either the Russian or Chinese revolutions. As a matter of fact, according to Marx's theory of history, it was not possible during his lifetime or the foreseeable future to establish a socialist society in Russia or China, either by violent revolution or by other means. Marx considered capitalism to be a transitional stage of social development bridging the gulf between feudalism and socialism: society had to go through the growing pains of capitalism before attaining its mature stage, socialism. Thus, he was not against capitalism as an historic development, any more than parents are against childhood and adolescence, for they realize these are necessary stages in a person's development. One cannot rightly say that Marx, who considered the proletariat and the capitalists to be two concomitant classes of capitalist society, advocated revolution by the proletariat against capitalists in either Russia or China; for during his time these countries were in the feudal stage of social development, the proletariat and capitalist classes not yet having come into existence in them. He expected capitalism to be supplanted by socialism first in countries such as England and the U.S.A., both having by his time reached that stage of development he termed capitalism.

If Marx were alive today, he would undoubtedly characterize the revolutions of Russia and China as upheavals leading individual societies from feudalism to capitalism. He would say the Soviet Union, through its industrial revolution of the last forty years, has become a capitalist society, with the inevitable creation within its borders of capitalist and proletariat classes and with imperialist investment of surplus in weaker, less developed lands. He would say, further, that in point of time the United States is much nearer to socialism than the Soviet Union, while the Soviet Union is much nearer to socialism than Red China.

152

Nevertheless, the apotheosis of Marx has been perpetuated in the tenets of the Communist Party, and his slogans and maxims remain sacrosanct in Russia. For example, Marx used the slogan "Dictatorship of the Proletariat" to characterize that society which would succeed capitalism in a society. The Communist Party of the Soviet Union claims that "Dictatorship of the Proletariat" accurately describes the mode of political life in their country. But "Dictatorship of the Proletariat" does not truly describe the Soviet Union's political structure as presently constituted. The "proletariat," really a euphemism for the Communist Party, which consists of only several million members, cannot truly be equated with the working class.

Analyzing the slogan "Dictatorship of the Proletariat," we see it has the same meaning as our American slogan, "Government by the People." Both are high-sounding slogans having no relation to reality, insofar as actual implementation is concerned. "Government by the People" is a political paralogism. In order for someone to rule, there must be another person who is ruled without ruling. When everyone rules, we have a state of anarchy: there is no government. Actually, the people rule in neither the United States nor the Soviet Union; however, in our country the people are at least able to choose some of their leaders from a limited slate of candidates.

The platform of the Communist Party consists of "interpretation" of the party's scriptural writings, not of the writings themselves. Similarly, our Supreme Court technically is supposed to implement the Constitution; in reality, it "interprets" it. This actually amounts to appending the Constitution. The appendages are legalized as "constitutional," without, however, being incorporated into the text of the Constitution; and these appendages become precedents for future legal cases as being in consonance with the letter and spirit of the original document, which is the official aegis

153

under which the government operates. But the very fact that nine intelligent men often cannot agree on the meaning of the Constitution as it applies to many present-day cases indicates there is nothing in it which can be applied to these cases: therefore, the rulings rendered in such cases are actually neither constitutional nor unconstitutional. Since there is nothing in the letter of the Constitution relating to these cases, the Supreme Court is forced to "interpret its spirit" and to "read between the lines." This is absolutely meaningless, for there is nothing between the lines but the blank paper; and the "spirit" is nothing more nor less than the mentality of the reader. A document has no spirit. And one can only presume, not read, between the lines.

In recent years it has become increasingly clear that the Communist organization has split into at least two national factions—the Soviet Communist Party and the Chinese Communist Party. The Albanian Communists have also broken away from the Soviet Party. Both the Albanian and Chinese Communist Parties claim to be the true interpreter of Marx, holding that the Soviet Communists are anti-Marxist. The following is a statement of the Central Committee of the Albanian Workers' Party, as reported in the press on October 21, 1961:

> By publicly attacking the Albanian Workers' Party, Nikita S. Khrushchev has in effect started an open attack against the unity of the international Communist and Workers' movements, against the unity of the Socialist camp. For this anti-Marxist act and all the consequences that may ensue from it, Nikita S. Khrushchev bears the full responsibility.

The chief disagreement between these national factions concerns the question of war between capitalist and socialist societies. Recent articles in *Pravda* castigate the "dogmatists" of Red China, who insist that war between the "imperialists" and "socialists" is inevitable. The "dogmatists" in turn label their detractors "revisionists." But the belief of the so-called "dogmatists" that war between capitalist and Communist nations is inevitable is completely at variance with Marx's theory of history. Marx conceived of the final triumph of Communism not as a resolution of conflict between sovereign nations but as the inevitable outcome of the struggle between the proletariat and the capitalists within individual capitalist states.

The year 1956 witnessed the beginning of the progressive deterioration of the world Communist movement into national factions which at times act in concert yet remain independent of each other. Along with the institutional revolution there has been an attitudinal revolution symbolized by the downgrading of Stalin. Before 1956 the Communists throughout the world thought of Marx, Lenin and Stalin as a kind of holy trinity of consubstantial spirit-essences. The de-Stalinization of Russia therefore constitutes a psychological revolution in the Communist mind comparable to what would occur in the Roman Catholic mind were the Pope suddenly to announce that Jesus is not really the Son of God.

Revisionism eventually breaks up every movement organized under the aegis of an alleged founder whose teachings are considered infallible. As times change, differences of opinion regarding the master's wishes result in the defection of factions, each claiming that it alone follows in his footsteps. Once this splitting process has begun, it is usually irreversible. The splintering of the defected factions into new groups follows inevitably, the revisionists of today becoming the dogmatists of tomorrow.

Splinter groups which are the offspring of schism in a great organization allegedly founded by an individual can be likened to lifeboats leaving a sinking vessel. While the mother ship goes down, the lifeboats, bearing her name and carrying a few of the original crew, ply their separate ways. If a lifeboat happens to pick up survivors from other sunken ships, the new personnel, if they are numerous enough and so inclined, might eventually wrest control of the ship from its original crew and change its course. Thus it comes about that "the scribes and the Pharisees sit in Moses' seat" (Matthew 23:2), and that Lenin, Stalin and Khrushchev in turn have sat in Marx's seat and drastically altered from its original course the movement founded in his name.

The allegory of the lifeboats leaving the mother ship applies also to the defection of the Protestants from the Roman Catholic Church, the Reformation being metaphorically a mutiny on the mother ship. The name "Jesus" is on all Protestant bows. And throughout the four centuries since the Reformation was initiated, the mother ship has been losing more and more of her crew through mutiny; ultimately she will lose all and sink.

Again, we must learn there is a difference between a person who belongs to an organization and agrees with the attitude on a given issue promulgated by that organization and a person who agrees with this opinion, yet does not belong to the organization.

Unfortunately, the paranoiac state of "anti-Communist" vigilanteism called McCarthyism which gripped our country a number of years ago, and still has not been completely eradicated, obscured the whole issue of anti-Communism by lumping together in one subversive category those who call themselves Marxists—Communists, socialists, Trotskyites, etc. —and even such people as freethinkers and atheists who do not even profess adherence to Marxism.

The great Communist spy scare during the heyday of the late U.S. Senator Joseph R. McCarthy was characterized by the widespread prevalence of a mental quirk psychiatrists call "the transference of identity." When there is a belief in

156

the existence of some real or imagined evil which is intangible or otherwise beyond the pale of physical counteraction, this evil is mentally projected into objects, animate or inanimate, which are tangible and vulnerable; and upon these scapegoats the mob unleashes its fury. This great truth of human psychology is illustrated by the aftermath of the Tokyo earthquake of 1923. The hysterical populace, searching for scapegoats to vent their fury upon, found them in the helpless minority of Koreans living in the city and slaughtered them by the thousands.

In the case of the Communist spy scare, the actual Communist Party members in the U.S. were too few and far between to provide widespread tangible personification of the unseen enemy, the Soviet Government. Consequently, the notion was put forth in the land that there were innumerable "Communist sympathizers" within our midst and that these people were even more dangerous than the known Communists. A cowardly method of slander was thus provided by which disgruntled, ambitious underlings could defame their organizational superiors; the envious untutored could draw even with their more educated neighbors; the multitudes of unwashed could malign their natural superiors; bigots could stir up racial and religious animosities; and crackpots could express their delusions with impunity. By late 1953 the country was in a fantastic state of mass paranoia, with the situation rapidly deteriorating into a stampede in which millions of people could have been trampled. This paranoia was symptomized in many ways, one of which was the frequent sighting of flying saucers, a phantasm the reality of which was believed in by millions.

Senator McCarthy was a Machiavellian who succeeded in developing for himself an aura of infallibility in the fight against Communism. By his personal magnetism he was able to unite a large portion of the dregs of American society, with the aim of throwing the country into chaos, thereby creating

157

a political vacuum leading to dictatorship with himself as *fuehrer*. Although McCarthy was too insincere to be a bigot, he paraphrased Hitler's words "fourteen years of treason under the Weimar Republic" with "twenty years of treason in the White House"; and after President Eisenhower congratulated the chairman of the Senate committee which had recommended his censure, he bitterly revised his diatribe to "twenty-one years of treason in the White House."

McCarthy's rallying cry was, in substance: "I am against Communism; he who is against Communism rally to my cause." The two-edged implication was that all those against Communism must necessarily be for McCarthy and all those opposed to him must necessarily be in favor of Communism. This kind of rhetoric is what Aquinas called the fallacy of the *"argumentum ad populum"* ("the argument to the people") and has been used from time immemorial by demagogues. For example, in the second century B.C.E., Mattathias, the father of Judas Maccabaeus and the organizer of the revolt against Antiochus Epiphanes in Palestine, coined the slogan, "He who is for God rally to my cause." The implication was that all those who rallied to his side were for God and all opposing him were against God.

The downfall of McCarthy, the inevitable result of his censure by the Senate, also destroyed the symbol which united his backers. Recently several attempts have been made by former McCarthy supporters to close ranks behind aspiring successors to the late Senator; however, the unity of these subversive factions, formerly held together by a cult of personality, has been irretrievably destroyed. The neo-McCarthyite movement is doomed to failure! There can be no doubt that ever since the censure of McCarthy the political pendulum in this country has been swinging in the direction of greater sanity; it is extremely unlikely that it will again swing in the wrong direction for at least another generation.

The basic problem in our country of the "internal Communist menace," which was handled with such stupidity and savagery by both officially constituted bodies and vigilante citizen groups, should properly have been stated as follows: "There is an organization calling itself the Communist Party extant in this country which has been acting in concert with the Soviet Government to subvert our government and society by boring from within. Therefore, let us find those people who are members of this organization and remove them from positions involving the national security." This should have been the complete statement of anti-Communism.

It is meaningful to talk about anti-Communism only in an institutional sense, for regardless of the fact that persons working under the orders of the Communist Party may be totally ignorant of the doctrine which is the canon of that organization, they are nonetheless tools of the Party. It is correct to call an individual Chinese soldier a Chinese Communist, even though he might never have heard of Karl Marx; therefore, to oppose that soldier is to oppose Chinese Communism, not Marxism.

The professed adherence or antagonism to Marxism is in many cases noministic. How many professed Marxists and anti-Marxists have read Marx? How many who know nothing about the writings of Marx nor consciously agree or disagree with his doctrines are called Marxists by their enemies? How many who consciously agree only in part with Marx are called Marxists? And how many who consciously agree in part with Marx call themselves anti-Marxists? If Marxism were an institution—as is the Communist Party— then the proper meaning of anti-Marxism would be opposition to that institution. But since the various institutions, including the Communist Party, which profess adherence to Marx—not to mention unaffiliated Marxists—are not corporately unified (indeed are often violently antagonistic

159

to each other), anti-Marxism cannot properly be equated with anti-Communism.

b) *The Roman Catholic Church*

Christendom is that area of the world in which the majority of the people belong to organizations known as Christian churches, each claiming it was founded by the entity Jesus, the protagonist of the writings comprising the New Testament. It is from these writings that these "followers of Christ" have called themselves "Christians," for this is the word the book uses to signify the followers of Christ. Although their interpretations of the New Testament are disparate, the Roman Catholics and Protestants generally think of each other as Christians, because of their common professed belief in the New Testament. All the Christian organizations profess their belief in the Old Testament also, but it is noteworthy that no Trinitarian Christian church is called the Church of Jehovah.

The Roman Catholics, whose church membership is the largest of any organization in Christendom, claim not only that their organization was founded by Jesus, but that he appointed his disciple Peter as his first vicegerent on earth: "Thou art Peter, and upon this rock I will build my church" (Matthew 16:18). Peter is alleged to have established the central headquarters of the true universal church (the word "catholic" means "universal") in Rome; thus the members of this organization call it the Roman Catholic Church. The Roman Catholics also say that the successive vicegerents of Christ's church, starting with Peter, have been chosen in accordance with the rules and regulations of this "Holy Apostolic Church." The vicegerent also has the function of

160

Bishop of Rome, and has come to be called "the Pope," an English perversion of the Italian *"Il Papa,"* meaning "the Father." The Roman Catholics thus claim that theirs is the one and only true church of Jesus, for the succession of its leaders can be retraced to Peter, who was appointed its first head by Jesus himself.

Non-Christians can argue that according to some verses in the New Testament Jesus did not establish a new church; that Judaism was the religion of the apostles even after Jesus was taken up to heaven. If Jesus had established a new church, why after his ascension did his followers return to the temple in Jerusalem to pray? "And it came to pass, while he blessed them, he was parted from them, and carried up into heaven. And they worshipped him, and returned to Jerusalem with great joy: And were continually in the temple, praising and blessing God" (Luke 24:51-53). At any rate, the command "Go not unto the Gentiles, and into any city of the Samaritans enter ye not" (Matthew 10:5) indicates that the thought of founding a new, universal faith did not enter Jesus' mind. The national exclusiveness of Jesus' ministry is substantiated by the verse "Christ was minister of the circumcision" (Romans 15:8), which contrasts him with Paul, the "minister to the Gentiles" (Romans 15:11). In view of the "circumcision" verse, "Go teach all nations" (Matthew 28:19) must have been a command to teach not Gentiles but Jews who even then were scattered in the Diaspora. According to his own words, Jesus disclaimed any intention of being an innovator or reformer: "Think not that I am come to destroy the law, or the prophets: I am not come to destroy, but to fulfill. For verily I say unto you, Till heaven and earth pass, one jot or one tittle shall in no wise pass from the law till all be fulfilled" (Matthew 5:18). He does not even credit himself with originating The Golden Rule: "Therefore all things whatsoever ye would that men should do to

161

you, do ye even so to them: *for this is the law and the prophets*" (Matthew 7:12).[1]

In *The See of Peter,* James T. Shotwell, professor of history at Columbia University, states: "The first definite statement which has come down to us that Peter and Paul founded the Roman Catholic Church is made by Dionysius of Corinth (*c.* 170 A.D.). We have no lists of the Bishops of Rome until about that period and those we have do not agree."

Many Protestant theologians assent to the claim of the Roman Catholics that Peter was the first head of Jesus' true church on earth, for this is supported by the account in Matthew of Jesus' own words: "Thou art Peter, and upon this rock I will build my church." But they contest the claim that the present-day Roman Catholic Church is the lineal organizational continuation of the original apostolic church headed by Peter, that Peter was titled "The Holy Father" and that he was the Bishop of Rome. They point out that the Apostle Paul, in his "Epistle to the Romans," greets and mentions twenty-six Christians in the church "at Rome," not the church "of Rome," but sends no greeting to Peter, who, according to Roman Catholic belief, should have been the Bishop of Rome at the time this epistle was written.

Some Protestants claim that Innocent I, Bishop of Rome between the years 402 and 417, was the first to say the Apostle Peter had been the first Bishop of Rome; that Leo I, Bishop of Rome between the years 440 and 461, was the first to interpret Matthew 16:18-19 as a commission given by Jesus to Peter to head the Church; that Jesus pointed to himself when he said "the rock"; that St. Chrysostom (305-407) said "the rock" was the faith of the confession; that St. Ambrose (337-397) said the rock was a confession of the universal faith; and that St. Jerome (340-420) and St. Augustine (354-430) interpreted "the rock" as Jesus.

Each Protestant apologist claims that at no time was all

[1]Italics mine.

162

of Christendom Roman Catholic; that his own church has continued without interruption from the time of Christ; that his church was not founded as a result of the Reformation, but that after the Reformation Roman Catholics defected *en masse* to the true church of Christ. Yet no one can contest the fact that the Roman Catholic Church is an institution with central headquarters in Rome, headed by the Bishop of Rome, who is also called the Pope.

Apart from its origin and unique organizational setup, how is the Roman Catholic Church defined by its own members? Here are a few definitions:

1. "The Church is the congregation of all baptized persons who hold the same true faith, the same sacrifice, and the same sacraments under the vicar of Christ on earth."

2. "The Church is the union of men with God in Christ."

3. "The Church is all the souls in heaven—The Church Triumphant; all the people on earth—The Church Militant; and all the souls in purgatory—The Church Suffering."

4. "The Church is the Mystical Body of Christ. Christ is the head and soul of the Mystical Body. The members are the individual cells of the visible body."

Are these definitions complete, or are they only partially descriptive, in the same sense, for example, that the definition of a horse as an animal having four legs is only partially descriptive? Are these definitions completely consistent with each other? For example, the third definition includes all existing souls who have not been condemned to hell—believers and nonbelievers, members and nonmembers of the visible institution, deceased and living persons. This definition conflicts with the first, which says that the Church consists of baptized persons, i.e., persons officially accepted as members of the "visible body."

The Roman Catholics speak of their institution as "Mother Church," as though it were a female monad having a mind of her own, which would exist even if all her human members deserted her. Thus they feel the Church is not responsible for the sins of its members.

When a business corporation is convicted of wrongdoing, its executive officers are held responsible for the actions of the corporation. The rank-and-file stockholders, who are technically partners in the business, are legally not responsible for the actions of the corporation. The rank-and-file member merely approves, disapproves or is ignorant of the corporation's actions.

But do we ever speak of a corporate entity as though its actions transcend the actions of all its members, including its chief executive officer, as though it were a monad in itself with prerogatives of its own? This is the way Roman Catholics speak of their church. If Christ is the head of the Church, why not speak of the actions of the Church as "his" rather than "her" actions? Furthermore, it is incongruous to speak of Christ at one moment as the soul of the Church and the next moment to speak of the Church as a possession of Christ —"His Church"—as though it were something extrinsic to himself. Is it not ridiculous to speak of a monad as possessing himself, alternately referring to him as "he" and to his possessed self as "she"?

Roscelin held that such a universal as "the Church" is a mere name, a nonexisting *"flatus vocis"* (like Father Time or Mother Nature), and that only the individual is real. In the sense that "the Church" is spoken of as a female monad, "Mother Church," he was right. But no one can deny that organizationally millions of individuals share an affiliation with this *"flatus vocis."*

Because of this affiliation, today the opinion is still widely held that a Roman Catholic is in some way accountable for such barbarisms as the Inquisition—which he perhaps never even heard of. That this opinion still exists is evident from bigoted literature which flooded the country before the last

164

presidential election, arguing that since Kennedy was a member of an institution which had sponsored the Inquisition, he was not fit to be President. However, it is fallacious to argue that a Protestant is more fit to be President than a Catholic on the grounds that the latter is a member of an organizaion having a longer history of infamy. One must remember that at the time of the Inquisition's inception, the Roman Catholic Church was the only religious organization of consequence in Europe, apart from that area of Spain occupied by the Arabs. Who is to say that if the Protestant churches had existed at that time, their behavior would have been more humane than the Roman Catholics'?

The Roman Catholics do not think of the heinous acts of individual Roman Catholics as being acts of Mother Church, who can do no wrong. But Rev. John A. O'Brien of Notre Dame University, in his pamphlet *The Truth About the Inquisition* states:

> The Church must, therefore, bear her share of responsibility for the proceedings of this tribunal, so many of whose actions were marked by cruelty and savagery. They have left stains on the pages of history and their somber shadow falls upon both crown and papacy and shows that their occupants were the children of their day.

What does Rev. O'Brien mean by his words, "The Church must bear her share of responsibility for the proceedings of this tribunal"? Does he mean that all members, past and present, are responsible for the "proceedings of this tribunal"? If so, he unwittingly plays into the hands of those who believe in the responsibility of all Catholics for the Inquisition. If, on the other hand, he is talking about the female monad of whom Christ is the head and soul, the conclusion is inescapable that Christ must bear responsibility

165

for the proceedings of the tribunal. For as Roman Catholics have put it, "As the invisible soul of His visible Church, it is Christ who governs."

Chapter 14

THE TEACHINGS OF
THE ROMAN CATHOLIC CHURCH

Many books and pamphlets written by Roman Catholics are stamped with the imprimatur (an insigne signifying official license by hierarchical authority for one or more Church members to publish a book and for other Catholics to read it). No imputation of the infallibility of the individual or corporate group publishing a book is implicit in its being stamped with the imprimatur. What is imputed to the book is freedom from error which could lead the faithful to believe doctrines contrary to Mother Church's teachings.

The Bible is one book Roman Catholics believe to be infallible. Also there are books called "catechisms" which allegedly interpret the word of God infallibly and simply for the laity. Roman Catholics, it is well known, generally read the catechisms more than they do the Bible. Therefore, the catechisms afford one a much better clue to the religious opinions of Roman Catholics than does the Bible.

The Bible is "the word of God." However, the Bible contains much contrary to teachings in the catechisms, notably the permissibility of divorce (see Deuteronomy, Chapter 24). No doubt the Roman Catholic clergy prefer that the laity be ignorant of conflict between Biblical and catechismic teachings. But they cannot openly prohibit reading of the

Bible, since this would bolster the Protestant charge that the Catholic clergy hide the Bible from the laity. Therefore, to discourage reading of the Bible, the Roman Catholic clergy must resort to a stratagem more subtle than forbidding it outright. They use the artifice of telling the laity that the salvation of one's soul does not depend on reading the Bible; and since the Bible is difficult to understand, it can be dangerously misleading to the layman who reads it without the help of a competent interpreter. The clergy's success with this stratagem is evidenced by the few Roman Catholic laymen who read the Bible. Indeed, the great majority of Roman Catholics have only a cursory knowledge of the Bible's contents, particularly of the Old Testament. On the other hand, the Protestant clergy encourage the reading of the Bible—for ever since the Reformation it has been used as divine refutation of Roman Catholic doctrine.

The Roman Catholics contend they "have the truth." Yet members of their clergy have publicly admitted that many Catholics are ignorant of what Mother Church teaches. How can an ignorant person "have the truth"? He certainly does not have the truth regarding things he is ignorant of, for "to have the truth" can only mean "to know."

The claim that the faithful are unanimous in matters of official Church teachings presupposes they are all not only conversant with the same oral and/or written teachings but that they understand them fully. This presupposition is erroneous, for as every teacher knows, the same words heard by all members of a class are comprehended in varying degrees of proficiency by different students. Indeed, it is a matter of everyday observation that words are far from being a completely accurate mode of communicating thought. And the fault is not always with individual incompetency. Word analysts and semanticists have shown that many words are ambiguous and that the structure of sentences, even when grammatically correct, is often illogical. In his *Essay Concern-*

168

ing Human Understanding, Locke observes with truth: "And it is merely about the signification of words that most of the disputes in the world are,—nay, even those that seem to be about things." Thus, even if it be true that the teachings of Mother Church have been put into word form and set down in books, the members of the Church, all being monads, are apt to interpret each teaching multifariously.

Teaching involves transmission and reception: the teacher and the taught. Which of Mother Church's members teach and which are taught? And how does a lay Roman Catholic who is apprehensive that a particular act he is contemplating may be sinful know what Mother Church teaches on this matter? Suppose, for example, he wants to know if it is a desecration of the Sabbath to play golf on Sunday. He cannot communicate directly with Mother Church (whoever she may be) and obviously he cannot ordinarily communicate with the Pope, the only infallible spokesman on matters of faith and morals. The bishops are said to be the teachers of the Church, for they are "the successors" of the apostles, whom Christ commanded: "Go ye into the world, and preach the gospel to every creature" (Mark 16:15). But it is not practicable for every Roman Catholic to learn Church teachings directly from a bishop. And as it is openly admitted that even bishops are fallible, how is the lay Catholic who consults his parish priest to know for certain whether he is hearing the teachings of the faith or the fallible opinion of one man? Father Leonard J. Feeney was excommunicated for teaching false doctrines. How then does this puzzled layman know that the priest he consults will not one day be excommunicated for having misled him on the question of playing golf on Sunday?

An article in the *New York Times* of January 8, 1964 illustrates the disagreement between Roman Catholics on questions of sin. It reports that Aloysius J. Welsh, Director of Pope Pius XII Institute of Social Education, said that the smoker committed a sin by "unnecessarily incurring a danger to his health."

"If a person is warned by a physician to stop smoking and fails to do so," Father Welsh said, "the sin is mortal. If he smokes only for pleasure or relaxation and fails to make a reasonable and continuing effort to quit, then he is committing at least a venial sin."

The *Times* article continues:

> Bishop Thomas K. Gorman, head of the Dallas-Fort Worth Roman Catholic Diocese, said he "wouldn't go along with most of what Father Welsh says.
>
> "I'm smoking a cigar right now and believe there is nothing fundamentally wrong. . . . That's not sin. I do believe a person directed to quit by a physician should do so because to continue would be harmful."

Father Welsh warns it is sinful to smoke against your doctor's orders. But suppose your doctor is mistaken in telling you that smoking is harming your health? In what way are you sinning by smoking?

In the Mosaic Law, sin was standardized—that is, all who were under the Law were under equal obligation to obey it in like manner and no special dispensations were to be granted to privileged persons.

But in the Roman Catholic Church the performance of certain acts is considered sinful when occurring in some locales, not sinful in others. For example, Cardinal Spellman, Archbishop of New York, declared it a sin for a Catholic of his diocese to see the motion picture, *Baby Doll*. However, Cardinal Cushing, Archbishop of Boston, did not. Thus a Catholic seeing this picture in New York was obliged to confess this sin; however, in Boston a Catholic could see the picture with a clear conscience. So we see that each bishop has autonomy on questions of sin within his diocese. A

170

Catholic disobeying his bishop is said to be guilty of the "sin of disobedience" even if the act he has committed is not prohibited in all other dioceses.

This principle of limited local autonomy by bishops in the matter of what is and what is not sinful has led to great confusion. For example, before the Puerto Rican national election of 1960, three Puerto Rican bishops issued a ban on voting for Governor Muñoz Marín. The pastor of the parish of San Juan publicly stated that Catholics who voted for Marín should not seek communion until they have confessed this "sin." However, on October 23, 1960, Cardinal Spellman said that Roman Catholic voters of Puerto Rico would not be sinning, nor would the Church penalize them if they voted contrary to the directive issued by the three Puerto Rican bishops. Shortly thereafter, an editorial in the Jesuit weekly publication *America* said that the U.S. Catholic remained "profoundly confused and embarrassed" by the action of the Bishop of Puerto Rico. Marín was subsequently re-elected. Having failed to intimidate the people, the bishops of Puerto Rico had no alternative but to retract the threat of excommunication against all who disobeyed their edict. In other words, God, whom bishops represent in their own dioceses, was intimidated by people to change His mind about what constituted a sinful act.

In Roman Catholicism there are also different standards of sin for the poor and the wealthy. For example, in spite of the fact that suicide is a "mortal sin," a millionaire named Clendenin Ryan, who killed himself on September 13, 1957, was given absolution. Priests took into consideration the fact that Mr. Ryan had been under the treatment of a psychiatrist, who said his patient suffered periods of depression.

But assuming that suicide is a mortal sin when committed by a sane person, how do we really know, in retrospect, that anyone who committed suicide was sane? It is axiomatic that only God can look into the soul.

Some say that in Ryan's case he repented before he died. Could this not be true in all cases of suicide? Why is it that extenuating circumstances are found only when suicide is committed by persons whose families contribute large sums of money to the Church?

Perhaps one reason suicide is a mortal sin is that such a sinner reduces Church membership and sets a dangerous precedent for others to follow. There is no Biblical basis for this doctrine. King Saul committed suicide, yet the Bible does not censure him for this act. Quite the contrary; it has immortalized David's eulogy of Saul (2 Samuel, Chapter 1).

The entire system of the confessional presupposes that each Catholic is infallible in matters of faith and morals, since he is supposed to confess all his sins. Obviously, he cannot do this unless he knows which of his acts are sinful. Some Catholics answer this by saying that Catholics do not have to be infallible to be absolved, because a priest absolves a sinner of all his sins, even of those the sinner does not confess because he does not realize they are sins. This absolution from all sins is a non-sequitur, for the prior condition for the forgiveness of a sin is repentance and a solemn resolution not to repeat it. If a person does not know a particular act of his is sinful, he can neither repent of it nor resolve not to repeat it. Thus, in matters of faith and morals, he *is* fallible.

A distinction should be drawn between "faith" and "the faith." When people talk about faith they are not necessarily referring to the tenets of a particular religion, but to the general proclivity of man for believing in events and monads of which he has no first-hand experience. Aquinas says, "Faith goes beyond opinion in that it has a firm adherence, but falls short of knowledge in that it does not have vision." By "vision" he probably means the evidence of the physical senses. Since faith "falls short of knowledge," it is manifest that a person's faith in a particular matter is mixed with doubt. In fact, faith and doubt are as inseparable

172

as the opposite poles of a magnet. When a person knows something is true, he neither believes nor doubts it.

The difference between "faith" and "belief" is that one believes many things which are distasteful to him, but has faith only in those things he hopes are true: "Faith is the substance of things hoped for, the evidence of things unseen" (Hebrews 11:1). Faith is thus one kind of belief.

Every Roman Catholic is said to have "the gift of faith" imparted through baptism. This "gift" enables one to acquire knowledge of and belief in the tenets comprising the faith. "Divine faith" is also used by Roman Catholics to signify a person's ability to acquire faith in "the faith." "Divine faith" and "the gift of faith" imparted to the new-born child through baptism are therefore the same. Obviously, a new-born child can have no more knowledge of the tenets of the institution into which he is being initiated without his consent than does a child born to cannibals in the Solomon Islands. If he had this knowledge, it would not be necessary to train him in "the faith."

In the case of an adult converted to Roman Catholicism, his "divine faith" was a prerequisite for his baptism. If baptism enables one to acquire faith in "the faith," then the adult converted to "the faith" before being baptized must have had an even greater gift than that imparted to the ordinary Catholic through baptism—namely, the gift of personal revelation.

There is, however, a Roman Catholic doctrine that a non-Catholic Christian who is sincere in his faith is really a member of the Church through "baptism by desire," even though he has not been baptized with "holy water." For his ignorance of the truth of the true faith is "invincible," not willful. A papal encyclical, *Out of the Church There Is No Salvation,* was issued many centuries ago when Roman Catholicism was the supreme religion in Europe. But since the power of the Roman Catholic clergy has been progressively

173

weakened by Protestantism, there is a tendency in modern times for the clergy to placate the non-Catholic with artifices such as "baptism by desire," which imply that even he can be saved if he is sincere.

It should be evident to rational infidels that baptism with water is actually nothing more than initiation into official Church membership, and that no intrinsic gift of faith is imparted to an individual by baptizing him. If he has any gift pertaining to Catholicism, it is the gift of circumstance. All beliefs, religious or otherwise, are acquired through environmental conditioning and the innate ability to learn from these external circumstances. The mind of an ordinary unbaptized person, if conditioned in the tenets of the Catholic faith, will digest these tenets just as fast as it would if this person had been baptized with "holy water"; and if the mind of a baptized person is conditioned in the tenets of a faith other than the Roman Catholic, he will believe those tenets, not the Roman Catholic tenets, just as though he had never been baptized. The celebrated case of Hildy McCoy, a child born to a Roman Catholic mother and baptized in "the faith," illustrates the speciousness of the doctrine of "divine faith." This child was adopted by Jewish foster parents and, being brought up in the Jewish faith, believes in it, not in Catholicism.

Every religion has this basic flaw: that it consists of a system of beliefs which the great majority of its adherents acquire through social conditioning rather than through personal revelation. Schopenhauer puts it humorously in his *Dialogue on Religion:*

> The Catholic clergy, for example, are fully convinced of the truth of all the tenets of their church, and so are the Protestant clergy of theirs, and both defend the principles of their creeds with equal zeal. And yet the conviction is governed merely by the country native to

174

each; to the South German ecclesiastic the truth of the Catholic dogma is quite obvious, to the North German, the Protestant. If, then, the convictions are based on objective reasons, the reasons must be climatic, and thrive, like plants, some only here, some only there.

If the Franks under Charles Martel had not in the year 732 repelled the Arab incursion east of the Pyrenees, all those who now profess their faith in Jesus Christ would probably be worshiping Allah.

The alleged bond between Catholics and Protestants is really only nominal, for the gulf between the Protestant and Catholic interpretations of the will of Jesus Christ is even wider than that between the Jews' interpretation of Jehovah's will and the Moslems' interpretation of Allah's will. The Reformation resulted from disputes between Catholics. It was not imposed on Europe from without; it came from the heart of Roman Catholic Christendom itself. Prior to the Reformation, the populace of each of those nations which was eventually to become preponderantly Protestant was almost completely Catholic. The fact that Protestants call God "Jesus Christ" is therefore indicative only of the early mental conditioning of the original reformers, not of any real bond between them and the Catholics.

The argument advanced by Roman Catholics that the multiplicity of Protestant denominations proves the speciousness of the Protestant claim to the legacy of Jesus Christ is untenable. For if one of these denominations happens to be the true church of Jesus Christ, all the other Christian churches, including the Roman Catholic, are false.

CONCLUSION

The fundamental question I have analyzed concerning the relation between monads is this: Is it possible for one who knows the name and history of a monad to feel emotion toward it if he does not know an entity of which it has been a part? For example, is it meaningful for one who knows the histories of his great-grandmother and great-great-grandmother to say he loves the former, but not the latter, unless he is able to distinguish between the two bodies with which these monads were joined in the distant past? If he has no mental picture of the two bodies, then it is as meaningless for him to say that he loves one monad but not the other as it is for a person born blind to say that he prefers a red rose to a white rose. Such a person may be taught to say a red rose is more beautiful than a white rose, but if both were set before him, he could identify the red rose only if it exuded a fragrance different from the white rose or if he were aware of some difference in configuration between the two species.

Actually, people unconsciously realize that you cannot love a monad unless it is joined with some physical body; this is why in many parts of the world they build statues to create a physical presence for god-monads.

Art historians well know that during the many centuries since Jesus is said to have walked the earth the conception of this entity has changed greatly. In his *Last Judgment*, Michelangelo painted Jesus as a muscular man. On the other hand, Rembrandt pictured him as frail and sensitive. In one version, Jesus is bold and assertive; in the other, ascetic and contemplative. Of all the representations of Jesus, which of them actually portray him so that we would know him were he to reappear in the physical guise of his first coming? Nobody knows.

The Jews rejected the Christian notion of God-become-man, for their entire religious history after their exodus from Egypt until the Babylonian Exile was pervaded by the struggle to extricate themselves from the belief in the corporeality of God. By the time of the Christian era they had long since completely spiritualized Him, so that no longer could they think of any living thing or similitude of a living thing as being joined with Him.

The Jews' concept of an incorporeal God and their projection of His presence from the precarious arena of human strife, the earth, to a heavenly sanctuary has served to perpetuate their religion with its nominal worship of Him by the name "Jehovah." For a spirit in heaven cannot be destroyed by the human hand; therefore it cannot be debunked in the human mind. To vindicate Jehovah's omnipotence, the power of the enemies of "the chosen people" has been rationalized as the instrumentality of his corrective chastisement—"the staff of the Lord's anger" (Isaiah 10:5-6).

Theoretically, Trinitarian Christians should speak the name "Jehovah" with a reverence equal to that with which they honor the name "Jesus," for Jehovah and Jesus are alleged to be consubstantial in spirit-essence. However, although in ceremonies of Trinitarian churches the words "the Father" are often spoken, the name "Jehovah" is never mentioned.

It is evident that the true reason the Trinitarian clergy shun the name "Jehovah" is that, first, the Jews do not believe in the divinity of the monad which was joined with the body of Jesus: consequently, if the Trinitarians were to call the

Father "Jehovah," this could be interpreted as a concession to Judaism without reciprocity on the part of the rival religion; second, use of two names to designate God could open the way to an eventual dichotomy of Christendom, each of the two rival factions preferring one name to the exclusion of the other.

Many of the Trinitarian clergymen try to implant in the minds of their flock the belief that the Son was really an innovator who abrogated the Father's teachings, that the Son was a personality different from, indeed superior to, the Father. Here is one way they accomplish this subtle brainwashing: Discussing materialism versus the life-of-the-spirit they will say, "Our Lord said, 'Man shall not live by bread alone.'" (By "our Lord" they invariably mean the Son in his human guise, never the Father.) But they try to avoid saying that "our Lord" was quoting Deuteronomy, which was written more than a thousand years before the reign of Herod, the age, according to the New Testament, in which Jesus was born. Although it may be truthful to say "our Lord" said this, it is only part of the truth. The purpose of this half-truth is "to kill two birds with one stone": to show (a) that Jesus was an innovator promulgating a doctrine which had never been preached before; and (b) that the Jews do not believe man does not live by bread alone, for they do not believe in Jesus. The belief is thus implanted in the minds of churchgoers that Christianity, advocating the life-of-the-spirit as opposed to materialism, is superior to Judaism.

Another New Testament teaching which Trinitarian clergymen claim to be an original teaching of Jesus, "Thou shalt love thy neighbor as thyself" (Matthew 19:10), is also a quotation from the Old Testament Law (Leviticus 19:18).

The value of a teaching such as "Love thy neighbor as thyself" would be neither more nor less valuable if it were originated by Gautama, Allah, Confucius or the devil himself. Christians, however, "accept" the teachings of Jesus

178

not because of the value of the teachings per se but because they believe the monad of the entity Jesus was the Son of God. The following passage in *Nathan the Wise* is a commentary on humanity's proneness to appraise the value of a teaching not because of the teaching's social and moral value but because of the reputation of its originator.

You do not know, you will not know the Christians:
Christianity, not manhood, is their pride.
E'en that from which their founder down has spiced
Their superstition with humanity,
'Tis not for the humanity they love it.
No; but because Christ taught, Christ practiced it.
Happy for them that he was so good a man!
Happy for them that they can trust his virtue!
His virtue? Not his virtue, but his name,
They say, shall spread abroad, and shall devour
And put to shame the names of all good men.
The name, the name is all their pride.

According to the Gospel text, to Jesus the practice of principles as a means of salvation took precedence over adherence to the cult of personality built around him. To the young man who wanted to inherit everlasting life in "the kingdom of heaven" he said, "Obey the commandments" and "Sell all your possessions" (Matthew 19:21), not "Believe in me, for I am your Lord and Savior." Belief in Christ as the means of salvation was evidently not Jesus' teaching but Paul's. Assuming Paul's prescription for salvation was the correct one, Jesus, when facing Pontius Pilate, had a glorious opportunity to save his adversary's soul by saying, "Believe in me." Was Jesus, the savior of all mankind, so callously indifferent to the salvation of Pontius Pilate's soul? To the latter's question, "Art thou the king of the Jews?" all he could reply was an evasive "Thou sayest it" (Mark 15:2). In today's parlance, this could be rendered as "You said it!" or oppositely, "That's what *you* say!"

In my discussion of Trinity I showed that in the Biblical exposition of the mental essences of Jehovah and Jesus, these essences not only are not consubstantial with each other but are inconsistent in themselves. But let us assume for the moment that the spirit-essences of Jehovah and Jesus as presented to us in the Bible are perfectly consistent in themselves and consubstantial with each other. Let us further assume that the writers of the Old Testament, calling God Jehovah, truly recorded the words He spoke before He manifested Himself as a man and that the writers of the New Testament truly recorded the words He spoke in the person of Jesus.

Often there is a great difference between comprehending a speech one has merely read and comprehending it by actually hearing the speaker deliver it. Inflection and modulation of the voice can modify and embellish the meaning of words; sometimes a sarcastic tone is used to convey a meaning directly opposite to that inferred from the same words when merely read. But neither the voice of Jehovah, heard by the prophets and a few other select persons, nor the voice of Jesus, heard by many ordinary people nineteen centuries ago, is heard by present-day Bible readers. Therefore, so far as the conveyance of God's parables and moral teachings is concerned, it would have made no difference to all the generations of believers born after Jesus ascended to heaven if God had remained only a spirit and continued to convey His message through interlocutors, as He had done prior to His incarnation as a man.

Throughout the centuries of its existence, the Roman Catholic Church has designated God by one and only one *nomen propium*—Jesus. The Protestant movement, as the word "Protestant" implies, was originally founded by defectors from the Roman Catholic Church. The reason these defectors advanced for leaving the Church was that it was not the true church of Jesus. Even if they had been so inclined, it would not have been feasible for any of them to organize a church under the aegis of a name other than Jesus. For their potential communicants, mainly from the Roman Catholic Church, had been thoroughly conditioned to call God "Jesus Christ." And so it has come about that the area of the world in whose religious life the Roman Catholic Church and churches which defected from it predominate is known as Christendom.

At the present time one hears much about the movement which aspires to a rapprochement between all religions calling themselves Christian. But although each of these Christian religions reveres the Bible as the word of God, each has its own favorite texts in that book which it draws on for its particular doctrinal apologetics. The doctrinal disagreement between the Protestant sects on the one hand and the Roman Catholic Church on the other is so great as to render eventual reunification under one church possible only through extensive revisions of canonized doctrine by each Christian church and the creation of a new cult of personality around Jesus. The eventual reunification of Christendom is therefore an extreme unlikelihood.

The "handwriting on the wall" indicates, rather, that those who are nominally Christians will come to realize the absurdity of confounding the material body of Jesus with the spirit-essence of God; also, of using a name as an "Open sesame," which they presently infer from verses such as "For when two or three are gathered together in my name, there am I in the midst of them" (Matthew 18:20). A human being or an animal can be trained to know its name so that it will know when it is being addressed. But God has no need of a name for Himself, for He knows when He is being addressed. Calling God by a name is therefore the result of the confounding of animal and divine expedients.

The signs of the times indicate that the teachings of future religions which will supplant those now extant in America will be free of any imputation of divine origin. The belief in the divine inspiration of the writers of the Bible will be discarded because of its innumerable inconsistencies and contradictions. Rather, the new religions will prescribe the best ethical and social precepts for better living which have been taught by the world's sages, without imputing divinity to any of them; these new religions will not quibble over the histories of "divine" personalities, whether of pure spirit or of spirit manifested in the flesh.

> Son of the morning, rise! Approach you here!
> Come—but molest not yon defenceless urn:
> Look on this spot—a nation's sepulchre!
> Abode of gods, whose shrines no longer burn.
> Even gods must yield—religions take their turn:
> 'Twas Jove's—'tis Mahomet's—and other creeds
> Will rise with other years, till man shall learn
> Vainly his incense soars, his victim bleeds;
> Poor child of Doubt and Death, whose hope is built
> On reeds.
>
> Lord Byron: *Childe Harold's Pilgrimage*

INDEX

Abdullah, King, 128
Abraham, 10, 50
Adonijah, 55
Aeschylus, 40
Ahaz, 63
Alexander the Great, 41, 116
Alexander Jannaeus, 93, 94
Ambrose, Saint, 162
Aquinas, Saint Thomas, 34, 158
Aristotle, 15
Arnold, Benedict, 76
Augustine, Saint, 162
Augustus Caesar, 62, 93

Bach, Johann Sebastian, 141
Bacon, Francis, 79
Bennett, Arnold, 76
Boccaccio, Giovanni, 39
Boyle, Reverend Joseph, 9
Buber, Martin, 109
Byron, 182

Calvin, John, 73
Carlyle, Thomas, 13
Chrysostom, Saint John, 90, 162
Constantine the Great, 42
Cromwell, Oliver, 10
Cromwell, Sir Thomas, 7
Cushing, Richard Cardinal, 8, 9, 170
Cyrus the Great, 58, 59

Dante, 117, 120
David, 55, 57, 58, 59, 69, 172
Davies, A. Powell, 93
Da Vinci, Leonardo, 15, 16
Descartes, Rene, 1
Dickens, Charles, 135

Edward I, 10
Eisenhower, President Dwight D., 95, 100, 158

Eisenhower, Major John S. D., 100
Eliezer, Rabbi, 104
Elizabeth, mother of John the Baptist, 12, 35, 60, 120
Elijah, 49, 60
Elizabeth II, 100
Epiphanius, Bishop of Salamis, 94
Esau, 4, 98
Eusebius, Bishop of Caesarea, 90
Ezekiel, 58

Feeney, Reverend Leonard J., 169
Feisal, King, 128
Ford, Henry, 75, 76
Frazer, Sir James, 24, 36, 38, 39, 97, 108
Fukuyama, Doctor Yashio, 150

Gautama Buddha, 96, 178
George III, 62
Geyer, Ludwig, 129
Goldwater, Barry, 129
Gorman, Bishop Thomas K., 170
Graham, Billy, 124

Hawthorne, Julian, 78
Herod the Great, 27, 67, 94, 178
Hezekiah, 26, 66, 67
Hillel, 59
Hitler, Adolph, 130, 150, 158
Holbein, Hans, 7
Homer, 30
Hosea, 68

Innocent I, Pope, 162
Irenaeus, Saint, 41
Isaac, 4, 10, 98
Isaiah I, 38, 56, 57
Isaiah II, 38, 56

183

Jacob, 4, 10, 38, 98
Jeremiah, 26, 31, 32, 114, 116
Jeroboam, 56
Jerome, Saint, 51, 52, 162
John XXIII, Pope, 100
John the Baptist, 12, 13, 59, 60, 120, 121, 122, 123, 124, 125
Johnson, President Lyndon B., 5, 7, 23, 48, 73
Jonah, 65
Josephus Flavius, 90, 91, 132
Josiah, 26
Judas Iscariot, 16, 91
Justin the Martyr, Saint, 19

Keller, Helen, 4
Khrushchev, Nikita, 154, 156
Kant, Immanuel, 147
Kierkegaard, Soren, 70
Kennedy, President John F., 165

Lazarus, 3
Leo I, Pope, 162
Lessing, Gotthold E., 23
Locke, John, 36, 112, 113, 169
Luther, Martin, 51, 59
Lynch, Reverend Oscar V., 110

Maimonides, 34, 103, 104
Malachi, 36, 37, 38, 60, 120
Mann, Thomas, 80
Marcion, 20
Marin, Governor Muñoz, 171
Marlowe, Christopher, 79
Martel, Charles, 175
Mary, mother of Jesus, 6, 67, 115, 116, 117, 120
Mattathias the Hasmonaean, 158
Marx, Karl, 151, 152, 153, 155, 159
McCarthy, Senator Joseph R., 156, 157, 158
McCoy, Hildy, 174
Micah, 57, 67
Michelangelo, 176
Montanus the Phrygian, 25

More, Saint Thomas, 7
Moses, 26, 27, 37, 38, 45, 48, 49, 54, 109, 138

Naomi, 23
Napoleon, 141
Nathan, 69
Nixon, Richard, 132

O'Brien, Reverend John A., 165
Origen, 90

Pascal, Blaise, 137
Paul the Apostle, Saint, 46, 71, 114, 129, 137, 151, 161, 162, 179
Perlman, Alfred E., 119, 125
Peter, Saint, 8, 69, 91, 145, 160, 161, 162
Philo, 89
Philomena, Saint, 8, 9, 82, 83, 84
Poe, Edgar Allan, 99
Pontius Pilate, 40, 179
Porres, Saint Martin De, 85
Pythagoras, 21

Rembrandt, 177
Richard III, 76, 77, 92
Roosevelt, President Franklin D., 76
Roscelin, 164
Ruth, 23
Ryan, Clendenin, 171, 172

Santa Claus, 92
Saul, 54, 55, 172
Savonarola, Girolamo, 85
Schopenhauer, Arthur, 89, 142, 174
Schubert, Franz, 6
Scott, Sir Walter, 143
Sennacherib, 66
Shakespeare, 10, 11, 76, 79, 80, 102
Sheen, Bishop Fulton J., 119
Shotwell, Professor James T., 162

Smith, W. Robertson, 29
Solomon, 26, 27, 55, 69
Spellman, Francis Cardinal, 170, 171
Spinoza, Benedict, 21, 141, 142
Stalin, Joseph, 155, 156
Storm, Tempest, 102
Strauss, Lewis, 101

Tacitus, 89
Tertullian, 25
Tolstoy, Count Leo, 144

Wagner, Richard, 129, 130
Washington, 62
Welsh, Reverend Aloysius J., 169, 170
Wilde, Oscar, 101

Xenophanes, 38

Zacharias, father of John the Baptist, 12, 35, 60
Zechariah, 111